The Hidden Grand Strategy

How America Engineers Wars To Weaken Russia And China

James E. Isham

Global East-West (GEW) London

Copyright © 2025 by James E. Isham

GEW Strategic Reports Series (Geopolitics)

Supervised by Hichem Karoui

Global East-West (GEW) london

All rights reserved.

No portion of this book may be reproduced in any form without written permission from the publisher or author, except as permitted by copyright law.

Contents

1. Introduction 1
   Understanding America's Dual Strategic Framework

2. The National Security Strategy vs. The Hidden Grand Strategy 21
   Conceptual Framework

3. Case Study I: Ukraine-Russia 41
   The Ukraine Conflict and Washington's Strategic Calculus

4. Enabling Kyiv 59
   U.S. Support, Alliance Dynamics, and European Burdens

5. Case Study II: East Asia Pivot 77
   Japan, China, and the Indo-Pacific Contest

6. Geopolitical Dynamics in the South China Sea 97
   U.S. Strategies and Chinese Perceptions of Containment

7. Proxy Fronts and Strategic Attrition 119
   Mechanisms of Balance-of-Power Politics

8. From Containment to 'Lean-Forward' 139
   Historical Evolution of U.S. Strategies

9. Ethical and Geopolitical Risks 151
   Escalation, Cohesion, and Moral Challenges

10. Conclusion 165
    Coherence and Danger in America's Hidden Grand Design

1
Introduction
Understanding America's Dual Strategic Framework

Summary of Strategic Frameworks: Meaning and Context

Strategic rationality underpinning frameworks is also a central issue in the analysis and conduct of world politics. For some time now, both nation-states and theorists have struggled to understand the impact of strategic paradigms on policy and more (Silove 2018). In American strategic thinking, deciphering these doctrines is critical for understanding the shifting contours of national security and foreign policy. Examining the underlying differences in strategic paradigms, it is evident that these are more than semantic terms: they represent a range of ideological moorings that have considerable weight in the making of decisions. As they navigate the dense terrain of strategic concepts, there are several guiding axioms, operating conceptions, and overarching goals that together make up what U.S. strategic thought encompasses. Within such frameworks, grand strategies/national security doctrines also take shape with their historical inheritances and topical challenges (Gaddis 2005). Second, the details of interagency collaboration and use of diplomatic, military, economic, and information instruments of power provide insights into how these constructs are translated into policy and practice (Biddle 2004).

Strategic linking and Admirals of the home front The elastic quality of strategic concepts is additionally evident in their use at home and abroad, with anomalous terms from two theaters—strategic paradigms—one national nested within another 'trailing' transnational—demonstrating that, as a metaphor for American statecraft, this one slips into gear as needed. Through the consideration of these schemes, one sees the point at which theory encounters actuality, and it enables us to appreciate more fully how America's international approach is based on both academic and kinetic foundations. It is the assertion of this paper that conceptual rigor is an integral component of well-informed and rational strategic thinking and conduct. The fusion of strategic paradigms into policy discourse requires accuracy in substance and appropriateness to circumstance so that the rhetoric and act of American statecraft resonate together constructively as they face current transnational challenges. At the same time, it is equally important to recognize the historical continuities and discontinuities in US strategic narratives, as well as how these change according to shifts in geopolitical contexts and new threats (Sestanovich 2014). In drawing lessons from these constantly changing paradigms of strategic thinking, we learn much about the complex dynamics that underpin their (re)construction as "strategy" and about institutional memory's role in strategic foresight for national security.

After Effects

The clash of strategic visions underscores a deep intellectual schism between traditions on the spectrum from continuity to change that creates a subversive challenge against available public policies in defense and foreign affairs at a time of revolutionary transformation juxtaposed against enduring strategic necessities.

In Context: The American Strategy Post Cold War

The post-Cold War world saw great changes in American strategic thinking as the United States tried to determine how it would fit into and position itself within a changed balance of power (Brands 2022). The U.S., a product of the bipolar system created by the Cold War, has moved into a multipolar world with changes in power structures and new strategic contests. This was also the period of a shift away from the containment doctrine that dominated in an earlier era, as policymakers sought to lay down a new strategic base for addressing those global challenges and opportunities. The fall of the Soviet Union and subsequent drift into unipolarity, propped by America's unmatched economic and military sway, forced a re-evaluation of existing power structures—resulting in a realignment of strategic concerns. This move centered the management of power and rule-setting rather than ideological contention, a complete reversal in American strategy (Porter 2020). In the 1990s, "democracy promotion," free markets, and human rights were touted as central themes of America's foreign policy—all in an attempt to maintain American dominance globally in spite of regional instabilities and newly assertive non-state actors.

The strategic environment for the United States experienced a dramatic upheaval with the attacks of September 11, 2001, and subsequent concentration on the war on terrorism and counterterrorism. This stage led to a reorientation in security and defense policy towards asymmetric threats emanating from transnational terrorist networks. Taken together, this combination enabled a more aggressive and involved policy that is focused on defeating radicalized ideologies and protecting American interests around the world. The focus was back on great power competition after 9/11, especially with the growing prominence of China and Russia as major competitors to US hegemony. A return to geopolitical rivalry highlighted the urgency for America to adopt strategies that reflect how different aspects of international relations—economic interdependence, technological change, and territorial disputes—are related. These factors in turn influenced the way that American statesmen considered these priorities and forced regular re-evaluation of foreign policy objectives vis-à-vis national security requirements. Hence, the emergent American strategy in the post-Cold War period represents an important node in U.S. foreign relations—one that clarifies across all levels of analysis (from international to domestic and sub-national) what went into shaping not only the results but also the requirements for readjustment from old U.S. strategic templates to new amid so many changeable international features.

Strategic Narratives: Officially Stated vs. Tacit Objectives

Strategic narratives are key to a nation's overall geopolitical strategy. It is inclusive of both the expressed objectives and the many times less explicit interests that drive a state's action in the world (Dueck 2006). Strategic narratives: from overview to intervention From the U.S. standpoint, strategic narratives are a confluence of public announcements and subtler but often more comprehensive strategic stakes.

The public face of American strategy is usually articulated in official statements, policy documents, and presidents' speeches—all decrying a vision of leadership for the globe dedicated to democratic principles and cooperative participation. Public communications like these are intended for both home and international audiences, as well as for the sake of defining U.S. principles and its concept of world security. Yet there is an intricate interplay of political, economic, and security factors behind such public declarations, which determines how a country will or won't act in reality. This distinction shapes a subtle negotiation of the explicit and implicit objectives that animate strategies.

Such narrative gaps can affect perceptions and coalitions, influencing how rivals frame strategic calculus in the great power competition (Yarhi-Milo 2018). This contradiction begs analysis to reveal the complex nature of U.S. foreign policy and its influence on international affairs. Finally, analysis of strategic narratives demands sensitive understanding about the shifts in the international system and changing power relations. Unraveling the dual face of American strategic narratives is an important task for policy practitioners, analysts, and foreign actors interested in understanding U.S. foreign policy behavior as well as its residual effects. This nuanced approach serves both to reveal the motivations and aspirations behind strategic steps and to expose the contradictions and tensions between overt statements and underlying strategic subtexts. This tension is difficult to resolve in order to forge a consistent set of diplomatic and military strategies that achieve a self-interest while sustaining regional stability and cooperation with foreign states (Experts react, 2025).

Key Driving Forces: Political, Economic, and Military Reasons

The twin threats within America's intricate strategic environment are driven by a number of political, economic, and military instigators. Politically, a mix of domestic demands, influences from abroad, and competition on the world stage also determines U.S. strategy. The strategic objectives of the nation can fluctuate, depending on political debates, election cycles, and party conflicts. Further, economic considerations are vitally important to American strategy: the nation's trade dependencies and emerging technology and resource distribution determine its global posture and ability to project power.

The symbiotic nature of economic interdependence informs and propels financial diplomacy, highlighting the strategic underpinning of economic calculus in statecraft. At the same time, the military dimension is crucial to understanding America's strategy. The dependence on military instruments, power projection capabilities, and armaments is unavoidable when talking about this balancing act. The linkage between military doctrine, deterrence policy, and operational design reveals once again the importance of military dynamics in conditioning America's two-pronged strategic orientation (Biddle 2004). Only by looking at these and other influences can we gain a holistic understanding of American strategy and how all these factors interact.

Actors and Decision Makers: Their Role, Contradiction

Within the complex terrain of America's dueling security paradigms, people and performers are innately tied to national security and foreign policy strategy. A range of actors and organizations—from senior government officials to private sector companies and nongovernmental organizations—participate in the development and implementation of strategic goals. Policy leaders for U.S. strategy, including the president, the National Security Council, and top members of Congress, make strategic decisions that frequently blend together domestic politics, international relations, and regional conditions. In this context, the conflicting relationships between different visions, priorities, and party interests need to be skillfully managed in order to facilitate agreement and coherence of action. Economics shows interest groups of businesses and corporations, banks and financial institutions, and trade and labor unions. Their assets, investments, and global operations overlap with national security interests, offering areas of cooperation but also potentially exploding points as they try to maintain a delicate balance between economic hopes and strategic necessities.

Furthermore, the national security apparatus, including DoD (as well as the combatant commands and defense industrial base), possesses substantial coercive influence over strategy on account of its resources, expertise, and warfighting capacity. And while competing visions of force projection, forward positioning, and technological innovation can lead to tensions and debates on resource allocation and risk management, they also demand coordination and dialogue among defense stakeholders. In addition to a patchwork of traditional government bodies, the strategic debate also receives important intellectual discipline, novel insight, and policy innovation from an extensive array of think tanks, universities, and research institutions (Van Evera 1997). "State of the field" is a tiresome phrase, one heard regularly—one might say ad nauseam—at APSA Annual Meetings and ISA Conventions, typically offering opportunities for new excitement and posturing, changes in priorities, and displays of hubris.

However, competing between actors who are expected to be more or less driven by the same motives—especially for international relations and political science departments—can in fact push towards different orientations and conflicts that make them fail in nesting into consolidated policy frames all possible innovations. Despite this mix of stakeholders, however, it is shared commitment that is key for reducing conflict and promoting joint actions to attain the strategic goals. Navigating these complexities demands careful management, transparency, and inclusivity on the part of all stakeholders—particularly policymakers—to ensure that U.S. strategy is informed by a balanced conversation about ideas, interests, and expertise as new directions are developed and implemented. Understanding the agents and frictions in this complex landscape can help to manage strategic choices, raise stakeholders' commitment levels, and mobilize a broad political constituency committed to securing American external interests.

Institutional Dynamics: The Departments, Agencies, and Think Tanks

National Security Strategy Formulation and Implementation Vis-A-Vis Institutional Dynamics In America's twin-layered strategy model, institutional dynamics play a crucial role in the development and implementation of national security strategy. This part explores the complex webs of organizations, such as departments, agencies, and think tanks with their respective differences that contribute constructively to the strategic landscape in question. There are think tanks with significant U.S. government influence at the highest levels of state-to-state policy and military balance (DoD, DoS, intelligence community). And each department has its own competencies and vantage points on national security strategy, which usually leads to lively discussions and trade-offs. The CIA, FBI, and NSA are intelligence agencies that bring significant collection and operational capabilities to bear in furtherance of a greater strategic mission. And the think tanks contribute to the strategic debate by providing independent analysis, policy advice, and conflicting points of view. These non-state entities are important repositories of expertise and also of independent thinking, influencing the development of military ideas. But the interactions between those entities are not always symbiotic. Interagency rivalries, bureaucratic resistance, and competing policy imperatives sometimes serve to prevent the coordination of a national security strategy, leading to wastefulness and conflicting policies.

Further, there can also exist conflicting institutional cultures and operating concepts that must be delicately managed and coordinated. Additionally, there is the delicate issue of balancing central coordination with decentralized execution processes, which necessitates an understanding of complex institutional dynamics. Dealing with these complexities requires stronger leadership, clear communication protocols, and strong interagency cooperation systems. This culture, based on mutual respect, common purpose, and a high level of transparency, is essential for minimizing institutional friction and ensuring strategic fits. To make the two parallel strategies and their joint relevance more cohesive and coordinated, the dynamics within these institutions can be acknowledged and considered. Ultimately, this section emphasizes the vital roles departments, agencies, and think tanks play in shaping and implementing American national security strategy by demonstrating the necessity of a well-run establishment and cooperative engagement across organizational lines.

Challenges in Framework Synchronization

The labyrinthine bureaucracies of the American state make it difficult for unwriteable strategic perspectives, which constantly contradict and disable each other, to be organized. Decisions and perspectives can vary so widely among political agencies and departments that a major challenge emerges. The intersecting national security, economic, and diplomatic issues at play make for a complex map that has to be negotiated in order to execute coherent strategies and policies. Differences in perception of global trends and risk identification among actors may create obstacles for harmonization to function. Politicization, bureaucratic stagnation, and resource management are part of the problem. Balance needs to be fiercely protected all the time to protect the higher interests of the nation. A key challenge has been adding new domains and technologies into the framework (e.g., Mazarr 2019). These rapid changes in cyber war, AI, and biotech are adding a new dimension to national security and foreign policy that constantly needs to adapt. The arrangements being coordinated in this more dynamic setting need to respond quickly, as well as having a strategic eye on potential future risks.

But striking this balance between long-term strategic planning and ad hoc crisis management is proving difficult. The requirement of forethought must coexist with the practicalities born in reaction and be managed, taking sideshows very much into account even as you strive to retain focus on overarching strategic goals. This fragile balance creates another level of challenge in the synchronization of frameworks. The diffusion of decision-making and the sharing of authority among a large number of actors give rise to further obstacles. For all various stakeholders and interests to be directed towards the common strategic guidelines, open communication channels, good procedures, and conflict of interest resolution are essential. Syncing up, first and foremost, requires the coherent alignment of operations, values, and narratives throughout the entire gamut of a nation's activity. The past issues can only be met through a coherent approach that reconciles antagonistic priorities, removes frictions between the governance bodies, and guarantees a homogeneous, rigorous, and systematic way of thinking.

Analytical Methods: Describing alternating frameworks

A range of pathways help decode and make sense of these complex layers that form America's twin strategic visions. These methods link abstract academic concepts to specific historical cases to let underlying assumptions, quandaries, and implications in the strategic fabric emerge (Van Evera 1997). One way to analyze is to compare official national security strategies of China with unofficial and usually unwritten types. This methodology demands careful scrutiny and comparison of official texts, pronouncements, speeches, and programs with secret actions and subterranean strategies. We can expose the covert connections between one and the other from our understanding of the gaps and overlaps in overt and covert elements of American strategic practice.

Another important way is the planning of scenarios and wargaming exercises, which are conducted to simulate theoretic crisis situations and possible conflicts. Such exercises would allow analysts to deduce those unspoken priorities and thresholds that underlie American strategy, laying down paths for intervention, coercion, or deterrence. Similarly, the network analysis can be used to map a complicated interplay of relationships, alliances, and dependencies that support the national security and strategic objectives. By mapping the sources of influence and resource flows in this network, analysts can then follow the pathways through which strategic priorities are transformed into action. In addition, real-life examples provide important views on the practice of both strategic approaches. Studying historical episodes of the United States' twofold or open-ended intentions also reveals shared patterns, vulnerabilities, and persistent contradictions in U.S. strategic practices/preferences. Finally, in terms of the narrative analysis methods and cognitive mapping discourse, they offer a way to clear up the narratives, symbols, and cultural logics that support dual strategic paradigms. We do not have a crystal ball to consult when it comes to teasing out Americans' strategic calculations; instead, at the urging of the Pentagon Papers' Daniel Ellsberg, who urged the Press Foundation to focus on dismantling official rhetoric and language through appeals for access to what it conceals, we work backwards away from what keeps America's ruling elites awake at night.

Case Illustrations: Current Policy and Action Relevance

The U.S. has been swimming against two currents in recent years, confronting a few big external challenges—and needing the full power of its multiple interlocking strategies to meet them. The U.S.'s involvement in the fighting in Ukraine serves as a prime example. The annexation of Crimea by Russia and the war in Eastern Ukraine are just two examples that reflect this American strategic logic in action. The strategy choices and courses of action that paved the way for Russia's actions in Crimea and for the fighting in Eastern Ukraine were taken by American policymakers. The case shows the flexibility of the dual-track U.S. strategy involving diplomatic engagement, economic sanctions, and military assistance to Ukraine in conjunction with European allies.

The East Asia Pivot is also a potent symptom of the American geopolitical ideal (Brands 2022). Comments The strategic shift towards the Indo-Pacific region, with China getting into tension mode with other neighboring countries, had made imperative the recalibration of alliances and enhanced military cooperation and joint engagements, besides participation in multilateral initiatives. This complex diplomacy, security, and economic juggling act suggest that the US not only responds strategically to changing regional power games but also understands that regional stability and balance of forces matter.

Furthermore, U.S. participation in Middle Eastern combat also sheds light on how its twin strategic building is applied. From involvement in wars in Iraq and Afghanistan to fighting extremist groups such as the Islamic State, the intricacies and trade-offs of US national security strategy—and by extension strategic priorities—are stark. The interdependence of fighting, spying, and talking is a reminder that US strategy is multi-dimensional in its full complexity and needs to be pursued by coordinating various policy instruments towards overarching strategic goals. The U.S. response to global challenges, like pandemic threats, climate change, and technological competition, similarly demonstrates the saliency of its dual strategic framework today. Rejecting the false choice of applying a one-size-fits-all approach to all potential adversaries and instead embracing efforts along an entire spectrum that includes international cooperation, technological innovation, and regulatory competition would bring alignment between our responses to these transnational threats and our values and interests. Together, these case examples effectively demonstrate how the U.S. has applied a combination of the two strategies in dealing with today's complex external environment. They also underscore that the capacity to operate on the international stage requires flexible and nuanced responses, based on a sophisticated assessment of how threats are evolving in different regions and in combination with global geopolitical trends. As the world continues to evolve, this dual prism will be key for framing U.S. foreign policy and defending American interests.

Significance for Future Policymaking

The examination of its two postwar strategic models and their present interpretation and deployment in policy and action provides us with indispensable insights into the shift of world geopolitics. We need to look at the importance of this platform for future policymaking, especially in uncertain times. While the world changes at an ever faster pace, American leaders need to learn from previous strategic efforts and plan a path that advances U.S. interests while promoting peace and prosperity beyond our borders. Key to the framework's implications for future policy agendas is its adaptive potential ability to respond flexibly to new challenges and opportunities. This article shows how politicians, by analyzing a variety of current cases and their policy implications, can improve their strategies for tackling today's security and diplomacy challenges. This flexibility gives the framework longevity and maintains its ability to adapt to changes in the world.

And the importance of this two-pronged strategic approach also lies in its ability to encourage multilateral cooperation and alliances. As the U.S. aspires to lead in global affairs, it can use the interactive aspects of these big ideas opportunistically, instead of simply responding to challenges and crises around with these ad hoc measures, while at the same time nurturing coalitions among like-minded nations on issues of mutual security and economic interests. It is a springboard for the construction of cooperative political strategies for joint security and collective prosperity in which strategic engagement and alliance-building play a central role. Another important dimension of its relevance is that it has the potential to incentivize ethical and responsible foreign policy decision-making (Yarhi-Milo 2018).

Integrating ethics into geopolitics, which is of an alethic character, turns merely factual insights into ethically filled ones. By culling information in this way, policymakers can make values-based decisions that serve national interests. Not only is it good for the legitimacy of U.S. policy, but it also leads over time to deeper and more principled engagement with the international community. Furthermore, the significance of this framework in policy is that it allows a combination of strategic autonomy and cooperative attempts to coordinate in responding sensibly to common problems. And the framework, for the United States as it lives in our multipolar global world of competition and interdependence, provides a way to think about how one can choreograph this tradeoff between self-reliance and reliance on others. By pursuing meaningful partnerships even as it retains strategic autonomy, American policy can navigate a path that serves U.S. national interests and global stability alike. The significance of America's two strategic postures cannot be overemphasized. Its flexibility, its ability to serve multilateral cooperation, its moral compass, and the possibility of combining strategic independence with interdependence make it an essential building block for developing good and efficient policies in a changing world. By adopting and utilizing the knowledge obtained from this framework, the next generation of leaders will be able to negotiate the shocks and challenges of global engagement with wisdom and finesse in order to protect peace, prosperity, and security.

***

1. Biddle, Stephen. *Military Power: Explaining Victory and Defeat in Modern Battle*. Princeton, NJ: Princeton University Press, 2004.
2. Brands, Hal. *The Twilight Struggle: What the Cold War Teaches Us about Great-Power Rivalry Today*. New Haven, CT: Yale University Press, 2022.
3. Dueck, Colin. *Reluctant Crusaders: Power, Culture, and Change in American Grand Strategy*. Princeton, NJ: Princeton University Press, 2006.
4. Gaddis, John Lewis. *Strategies of Containment: A Critical Appraisal of American National Security Policy during the Cold War*. Revised and Expanded ed. New York: Oxford University Press, 2005.
5. Mazarr, Michael J. *The Folly of Arms Control: Why Peace Requires a New Strategy*. New York: PublicAffairs, 2019.

6. Porter, Patrick. *The False Promise of Liberal Order: Nostalgia, Delusion, and the Rise of Trump*. Cambridge: Polity Press, 2020.

7. Sestanovich, Stephen. *Maximalist: America in the World from Truman to Obama*. New York: Alfred A. Knopf, 2014.

8. Silove, Nina. "Beyond the Buzzword: The Three Meanings of 'Grand Strategy.'" *Security Studies* 27, no. 1 (2018): 27–57.

9. Van Evera, Stephen. *Guide to Methods for Students of Political Science*. Ithaca, NY: Cornell University Press, 1997.

10. Yarhi-Milo, Keren.** *Who Fights for Reputation: The Psychology of Leaders in International Conflict*. Princeton, NJ: Princeton University Press, 2018.

Online:

11. Experts react: What Trump's National Security Strategy means for US foreign policy - Atlantic Council. (n.d.). Retrieved December 7, 2025, from https://www.atlanticcouncil.org/blogs/new-atlanticist/experts-react/experts-react-what-trumps-national-security-strategy-means-for-us-foreign-policy/

2
The National Security Strategy vs. The Hidden Grand Strategy
Conceptual Framework

National Security Strategy Distinguished

The National Security Strategy (NSS) of the United States represents an extensive backdrop to which the US conducts efforts to safeguard its interests and ensure world stability. At the heart of the NSS is the concept of securing national security by blending diplomatic, military, economic, and informational tools of power (Biddle 2004). The approach aims to safeguard a rules-based international system, grounded in democracy, human rights, and market economies, from potential threats by either state or non-state actors. The NSS was born in the aftermath of World War II at a time when the United States did a tremendous deal to help found key multilateral institutions and partnerships. America's strategic constructs have, however, evolved with geopolitical realities, technological capabilities, and threat environments over a period of time, which demanded frequent changes in the way strategy concepts have been conceived and applied (Gaddis 2005).

The key element of the NSS is the expression of grand strategic goals that favor democratic governance, free trade and fair trade, climate change, fighting terrorism, and WMD proliferation. The NSS is a whole-of-government document, calling for coordination across branches and agencies to address the complex problems associated with national security. It also emphasizes the need to involve allies and partners in shared endeavors, given that international challenges are interlinked and solutions must be found together. Ultimately, the purpose of the NSS is to have a clear vision of how America should act in the world, which will guide policy development, resource control, and alliance ripple effects. The NSS therefore operates as a compass, guiding through the underbrush of international relations while reconciling domestic positions and seeking to bring about stability and prosperity worldwide.

Background: The Transformation of America's Strategic Doctrines

The historical development of the United States' strategic paradigms is a combination of geopolitical transformations, technological development, and the recasting of its own ideological approach. Its development dates back to the birth of the nation, when the framers of the U.S. Constitution were concerned with questions about national security and interstate relations. America's strategic posture has altered substantially over time in ways that reflect the domestic and international contexts (Sestanovich 2014).

But in the immediate wake of World War II, with Cold War tensions applying enormous pressure to U.S. strategic planning, a new look at American priorities would lead to new ways of thinking about containment and deterrence---two of the defining terms of that era (Brands 2022). The end of the Cold War was a unipolar moment for America, which rose to take a dominant position globally and adapted her strategies accordingly. Although the post-9/11 era led to a paradigm shift, rising counterterrorism and homeland security became primary national security considerations. Moreover, the emergence of disruptive technologies and heightened global interconnectedness has necessitated a periodic recalibration in America's strategic frameworks to effectively respond to evolving threats and opportunities (Mazarr 2019).

The Monroe Doctrine, the Truman Doctrine, the Nixon Doctrine, and the Bush Doctrine are all examples of how the world has changed over time and how each age has had its own set of rules or policies. The relevance of these defining episodes and the reconfiguration of US national strategy demonstrate how to adjust the balance in an evolving world of new challenges. It is through examination of shifts in the underlying strategic narratives guiding America that we can gain rich insights into the interaction between national identity, security imperatives, and international behavior (Dueck 2006). America's Rise to Globalism The world faces significant pressure in its international security dimensions, spanning a wide range of shared interests and values.

Architects and Thinkers in U.S. Strategic Policy

Key U.S. strategic policy architects and contributors have profoundly shaped the country's national security themes, marching ideas from thought to policy into action. By virtue of their knowledge, vision, and stewardship, these retired men have played a central role in shaping the themes that underpin American strategic policy. One such example is George F. Kennan, a well-known practitioner and theorist whose original design of the policy of containment in the Cold War continues to shape American foreign policy and grand strategy (Gaddis 2005). The instinct to avoid overreacting and Kennan's call for an intelligent long-term response to the challenge posed by Soviet expansionism was a significant intellectual influence on post-war U.S. strategic thinking.

Another influential personality Kissinger, who is an icon of realpolitik and a practitioner of pragmatism in foreign policy, had profound implications on US grand strategy during his time as National Security Advisor (1969--1975) and Secretary of State. His geopolitical perspicacity and diplomatic initiatives in seminal theaters such as China and the Soviet Union remain highly relevant to today's U.S. strategic posture. The intellectual contributions of these strategic architects emphasize the enduring influence of outstanding minds on the development of American grand strategy and render the complicated dynamic between "intellectual rigor, statesmanship, and context" immediately evident.

More than just the work of individual contributors, influential think tanks and academia---including the likes of the Council on Foreign Relations, the RAND Corporation, and Harvard's Belfer Center for Science and International Affairs---have long served as hatcheries of new battlefield strategy ideas (Van Evera 1997). These institutions have nurtured intellectual streams that informed U.S. strategic policy making by not only adding variety to the debate but also different ways of evaluating strategies and tactics. And the interaction between practitioners and academics has been a dynamic environment---informing, sharpening, and even challenging U.S. strategy. The legacy of these architects and the thought leaders who followed continues into the 21st century, serving as a reference point for understanding today's complex global strategic environment and reminding us of the enduring importance of bold thinking in devising U.S. strategy.

The contents of the Official National Security Strategy

The official National Security Strategy (NSS) of the United States is published each time a new president enters office, and it defines the administration's approach to ensuring national security. Each integral part of the strategy paper shapes the country's position in international matters. A cornerstone of the NSS is to review China's present and future threats to national security, and in so doing, a comprehensive review needs to be done involving geopolitical challenges, tech advances, economic vulnerabilities, and non-traditional risks, including pandemics and climate change. The NSS establishes a foundation for future actions and resource allocation by defining and ranking these threats.

Another indispensable part of the NSS is the expression of national interests and values above all. Articulating these principles is a lodestar for foreign policy decision-making and helps focus multiple agencies and departments around common goals. The NSS also assesses the means to safeguard national security tools and instruments, including diplomatic sources, economic actions, military forces, and intelligence activities. The NSS also details the administration's methodology for partnership and alliances, stressing the need to work together on global issues.

Beyond that, the NSS speaks to the economic foundations of national security, acknowledging even an autarkic power's (e.g., Iran's) need for a well-functioning economy to sustain geopolitical influence. It underscores trade, investment, innovation, and energy security policies as part of the larger national security agenda. Finally, the NSS emphasizes the importance of preserving and improving the resilience of critical infrastructure, cyber network defense, and key institutions in an environment where threats may change over time. These actions would also entail steps to strengthen defenses against cyberattack, safeguard critical supply chains, and guarantee the functioning of government amid a catastrophe. Through the synthesis of these disparate elements, the National Security Strategy is designed to serve as a kind of blueprint by which decision-making can be coordinated between different parts of government while also projecting consistency and coherence in U.S. concerns and goals on the world stage.

Revealing the Concealed Grand Strategy: An Analytical Overview

The notion of a "hidden grand strategy" has increasingly captured the attention of analysts in academia and policy circles, who seek to transcend the more overt, publicly articulated strategic ends that predicate U.S. foreign and national security policies (Dueck 2006). A clear-eyed look at this stratagem, this secret "grand strategy," reveals a complex tangle of goals, partnerships, and machinations that directs America's place in the world. The analysis in this context involves an examination of the grey area that exists between what is officially a national security strategy and what may be strategically covert or tacit policy devised by the U.S. government.

Deciphering the discreet grand strategy demands a multi-dimensional look at history, military bureaucracy, and geopolitics. An examination of U.S. interventions, military basing, diplomatic relations, and economic relations reveals an unspoken geopolitical blueprint that goes beyond traditional national security doctrines. Moreover, reading this hidden game requires a contrast between the narratives of official statements and factual policies; thus, it reflects on the clandestine aspects of U.S. statecraft (Yarhi-Milo 2018).

Understanding the covert grand strategy will be crucial for policymakers, strategists, and diplomats called upon to bring coherence to our increasingly bewildering world. It offers sobering reminders as well as practical lessons for preemptive actions, diplomatic exchanges, and strategic rebalancings that can further national interests while dampening adversaries' animosities. Moreover, understanding the acutely obscured grand strategy can provide a more subtle and sophisticated understanding of the balance of power, alliance arrangements, and geopolitical rifts in the contemporary international order. This analytic survey is designed to bring to light the strategic and functional mechanics of America's "secret" grand strategy, thereby tasking readers to question the obscured forces that define its global position.

Cross-analysis: contrasts and similarities

A comparative reading of the National Security Strategy and its sibling, the Hidden Grand Strategy, suggests complex interactions between divergences and convergences (Silove 2018). The implementation of both strategies exhibits discrepancies in transparency and openness. Must also submit a plan...) The foreknown is evident from the inward direct agreement of their treasonable pretenses with the public oath and avowed resolution (in other cases) before mentioned. Hidden grand strategy, by contrast, is a vague concept usually involving subtle actions and diplomatic gambits that can be difficult to prove actually exist. This disjunction reflects the complex and sometimes contradictory character of US strategic policy and raises questions about how explicit programs that signal resolve can be interlinked with more clandestine activities to serve larger strategic goals.

However, we can observe some significant similarities between the two approaches. Ultimately, the broader objective of protecting national interests, maintaining global stability, and promoting American influence drives both sets of rules. While their means and processes vary, the raw objectives hint at a vital agreement of ideas. In this sense, the comparative analysis is relevant to showing the convergence in geographical and thematic focus between both strategies. Whether floating above local flashpoints or a global menace, the convergence of concern suggests that Trump has a cohesive and unified approach to his strategies. These convergences underline the interconnectedness of different strategic aspects and the synergy effects arising from a complementary policy design.

Finally, a thought-provoking contrast underscores the complementary nature of these approaches. The preemptive retention of certain qualitative capabilities posited by the NSS complements and contrasts with the quiet maneuvers complementary to the HGS, ultimately offering a synergistic, offsetting interaction between strategy at home and abroad. One method to gain such insights is through understanding and explaining the differences and similarities as they evolve between these two strategic paradigms among policymakers and scholars alike in the complexities of America's strategic calculus. This examination will facilitate further development of a balanced approach that optimizes the value of both concepts and makes our overall strategy more effective and less susceptible to exploitation.

Decision-Making Mechanisms: From Theory to Practice

The purpose of this chapter is to examine the complex subject of translating theory at the strategic level into operational effects within America's bipolar strategic edifice. Complex interactions shape decision-making processes, including geopolitical dynamics, technological developments, national political interests, and evolving global threats. Policymakers and field generals must adopt a more nuanced approach to policymaking, carefully navigating the tension between the National Security Strategy and the Secret Grand Strategy.

The tension between these two approaches and the ways they complement each other is key to understanding how decisions get made at the highest levels of leadership. Whether it is the preparation of diplomatic proposals, the authorization of military operations, or the negotiation of international agreements, we think that decision-making is structured according to underlying priorities and trade-offs stemming from both schemas. Readers are provided with historical context to analyze key points in U.S. foreign policy decision-making and the permanent influence of past choices on current strategic needs (Sestanovich 2014).

Furthermore, the study of cases allows for useful lessons in applying strategic principles and demonstrates these through vivid examples of good and bad strategy. From the

Cuban Missile Crisis to the War on Terror, each reveals a thorny problem that has not yet been solved---one we seem resigned to repeatedly encounter in some form or another every time our nation must translate strategy into action. Moreover, looking at the organizational forms and institutional procedures through which decisions are made provides us a bottom-up understanding of bureaucratic dynamics and outcomes. Describing the functions of key players such as executive agencies, defense departments, intelligence agencies, and legislators, this section highlights the complex dynamics behind decision-making.

Moreover, the adaptability of decision-making to changing international circumstances emphasizes the need for agility and forward-thinking in planning for an unpredictable world. Ultimately, closing the gap between theory and practice demands a serious investigation of these cognitive, institutional, and contextual factors in terms of how they influence U.S. decision-making and can offer an encompassing analytical framework through which to make sense of the complexities of strategy implementation in America's diverse strategic terrain.

Symbiosis or Conflict? Interactions between Strategies

The tension between the National Security Strategy (NSS) and HGS results, therefore, in a situation of dynamic relationships that range from symbiosis to conflict---it is not just one or the other. At the heart of this complex relationship is the issue of alignment: how much do the goals and means articulated in the NSS align with those defined by HGS above and beyond? Are they distinct?

Resource distribution is one domain where these interactive effects manifest. While the NSS contains budget figures or force deployments in response to immediate security needs, the HGS makes an imprint on strategic investment and international positioning over time. A delicate balance between temporary imperatives and persistent strategic interests is required due to this confluence. When the two are in tension, conflicting priorities may arise, necessitating a delicate balance between short-term considerations and long-term goals (Porter 2020).

Furthermore, a temporal component complicates the interaction dynamics. The NSS, with its focus on imminent threats and exigencies, functions in a shorter-term orientation that can overshadow the longer temporal timeframe of the HGS. Conflict risk arises when indignation and ad hoc responses to NSS dictates limit the long-term pursuit of grand strategic goals. It is necessary to consider the possible mechanisms for addressing such conflicts and promoting coherence between immediate security concerns and strategic perspectives over time.

In practice, the interplay between NSS and HGS is evident at every stage of formulating and executing national security policy. While the NSS formulates strategies for specific current issues, the HSG establishes the fundamental principles that guide U.S. actions in global affairs. This is the critical juncture where tactical decisions mirror overarching strategy, grounded in a robust foundation of fundamental principles---a synergy between immediate and long-term actions. The absence of this alignment risks sowing confusion and discord in American strategic behavior.

Furthermore, the international arena serves as a testing ground for the potential compatibility of the NSS with the HGS. The complex interrelationship between these strategic blueprints shapes the responses of friends and foes to U.S. statements of policy and actions. Cohesion in messages and activities is critically important toward presenting a consolidating front, increasing deterrence power, and increasing one party's influence in the relationship between nations. At the same time, however, dissonance/complementarity also can represent lack of clarity and inconsistency, which may challenge US credibility and strategic leverage.

The interfaces between the NSS and HGS are challenging to navigate, requiring deft diplomacy and strategic vision---and the willpower not only to square short-term security demands but also long-term grand strategies. Skillfully balancing this ever-present tension is critically important if policy members are to create a coherent and effective strategic vision that matches existing short-term realities with long-term national interests.

Impact on Global Stability: Implications for Allies and Adversaries

The impact of the two U.S. strategic paradigms on global stability is profound and has wide-ranging implications for both allies and adversaries. Comprehending the impact of these mechanisms is fundamental to managing the intricate global politics in the 21st century. Allies, for their part, are likely to consider the balance---or tension---between the National Security Strategy and the Hidden Grand Strategy to be a central input into their own strategic calculus (Yarhi-Milo 2018). The convergence between the U.S. strategic goals and its actions, whether or not there is a gap due to perfectly aligned intentions, can either fortify or undermine the security and economic interests of its allies. In addition, the predictability and coherence of U.S. strategic behavior has a direct impact on the confidence and trust that allies have in U.S. leadership, which affects alliance cohesiveness and cooperation.

For our enemies, a keen insight into the interdependency of the overt and covert strategies is necessary for them to preempt and react to U.S. moves. These subtleties reinforce their respect and anticipation of sensitive U.S. interests on the one hand, as well as inform them of potential tactical opportunities to probe for divergences between U.S. declaratory policy and actual policymaking so that they might exploit such discrepancies if they think it worthwhile if ever those differences become favorable to their objectives. Furthermore, the gap between U.S. priorities and actual strategic pursuits when calculated offers results related to regional wars, armament competitions, and ideological clashes. The convergence or divergence of the twin strategies ripples through the international system, influencing power and conflict balances and creating opportunities for peaceful dispute resolution.

The implications of America's unstated---and stated---postures regarding general multilateralism, globalization, and regional integration are significant and should not be overlooked. De Myth Understanding the implications of dual U.S. strategies for global stability creates possibilities for constructive engagement, risk reduction, and development of cooperative security structures. Appreciating the complex relationship between NSS and HGS enriches our understanding of this elaborate network of consequences, highlighting each one's stakes and respective pathways that ultimately distill worldwide stability for everybody participating in world politics.

The Way Forward: Synthesis of Strategies and Enculturation of a Unified National Vision

In conclusion, linking the National Security Strategy to the notion of a hidden grand strategy is critical for building a coherent sense of national purpose in the United States (Silove 2018). The consequences of these linked strategies for global stability underscore the need to develop a more comprehensive and consistent approach that balances domestic imperatives with international concerns. Such an integrated approach requires a coherent blending of policy goals, resource distribution, and decision-making processes from national security through grand strategic endeavors.

A common vision cannot be reached without the involvement of multiple stakeholders such as politicians, military figures, intelligence officers, diplomats, and civil society. An understanding of the interaction of conventional state-centric mechanisms with nascent non-state challenges (e.g., cyber security, transnational terrorism, and climate change), which may not demand a traditional or exclusive approach (Mazarr 2019). A proactive melding of the National Security Strategy with the Hidden Grand Strategy can improve America's abilities to navigate changing currents in world politics and ensure its resilience and efficacy on a global scale.

This integrative paradigm takes into account the balance between exigencies of the short run and requirements of long-term strategy, our institutional agility as well as our core national interests, and strategic agility in dealing with complex security dilemmas. Moreover, a fulsome approach fosters coherence in message and conduct, sending allies and adversaries alike the clear image of a unified and credible actor. In so doing, the United States will not only provide an overarching frame that integrates NSS and the Hidden Grand Strategy into a more coherent national purpose but also realize its potential as primus inter pares in shaping the emerging world order, keeping global peace and stability, and promoting universal values and norms. This conclusion underscores the necessity of well-considered and flexible mechanisms fostering alignment of disparate strategic streams and the cultivation of a strong national position in the face of prevailing altering geopolitical dynamics.

***

Biddle, Stephen. 2004. *Military Power: Explaining Victory and Defeat in Modern Battle*. Princeton, NJ: Princeton University Press.

Brands, Hal. 2022. *The Twilight Struggle: What the Cold War Teaches Us about Great-Power Rivalry Today*. New Haven, CT: Yale University Press.

Dueck, Colin. 2006. *Reluctant Crusaders: Power, Culture, and Change in American Grand Strategy*. Princeton, NJ: Princeton University Press.

Gaddis, John Lewis. 2005. *Strategies of Containment: A Critical Appraisal of American National Security Policy during the Cold War*. Revised and Expanded ed. New York: Oxford University Press.

Mazarr, Michael J. 2019. *The Folly of Arms Control: Why Peace Requires a New Strategy*. New York: PublicAffairs.

Porter, Patrick. 2020. *The False Promise of Liberal Order: Nostalgia, Delusion, and the Rise of Trump*. Cambridge:

Polity Press.

Sestanovich, Stephen. 2014. *Maximalist: America in the World from Truman to Obama*. New York: Alfred A. Knopf.

Silove, Nina. 2018. "Beyond the Buzzword: The Three Meanings of 'Grand Strategy.'" *Security Studies* 27 (1): 27–57.

Van Evera, Stephen. 1997. *Guide to Methods for Students of Political Science*. Ithaca, NY: Cornell University Press.

Yarhi-Milo, Keren. 2018. *Who Fights for Reputation: The Psychology of Leaders in International Conflict*. Princeton, NJ: Princeton University Press.

3
Case Study I: Ukraine–Russia
The Ukraine Conflict and Washington's Strategic Calculus

Historical Context: The Roots of the Ukraine Conflict and Its First Phases

Roots of the Ukraine Conflict The roots of the armed conflict in the Ukraine run deep and are steeped in centuries of historical and geopolitical as well as ethnic machinations. Its historical association with Russia and the other states of Europe has in large part defined its identity and political development. The 1991 dissolution of the Soviet Union became a defining moment for Ukraine as it began to emerge from its own sovereignty and used this new independence to create an identity in the global context. Yet the lasting remnants of Soviet influence and economic relations continued to inform Ukraine's domestic politics and foreign policy. Ukraine's geostrategic location in between Europe and Russia has seen an increase in its geopolitical importance, drawing in several regional and global powers to meet their competing interests (Brands 2022).

One cannot understand Ukraine's past posture without acknowledging its internal cultural and linguistic fissures, particularly between the Ukrainian-speaking west and the Russian-speaking east and south. This division, along with opposing historical narratives and divergent social aspirations, has made governance and national unity difficult. At the onset of the conflict, there were numerous political changes and upheavals, such as the annexation of Crimea by Russia in 2014 and waves of demonstrations that turned into protests, like during the Euromaidan and Orange Revolution protests. They were sparked by widespread frustration with corruption, governance, and Ukraine's geopolitical position, leading to the overthrow of pro-Russian leaders in favor of closer links with the European Union. Russia's subsequent annexation of Crimea in 2014 and the emergence of separatist movements in eastern Ukraine only escalated tensions, resulting in a proxy war that reverberated across the world. As such, the backstory of the Ukraine war paints a complex picture of identity and ambition, power and resistance, providing an alternately local, regional, and international frame that continues to shape its trajectory.

Interests: U.S. Goals and Motivation in the Region

The US interest in the Ukraine crisis is based on a series of strategic interests and goals that are rooted in its broader geostrategic agenda. Key U.S. objectives also involve supporting the international order and norms, especially those surrounding territorial integrity and sovereignty. Thereby upholding a rules-based global order, the U.S. is designed to avoid one-sided changes in borders and to discourage the use of force for territorial gains (Porter 2020). This is consistent with the end-state of promoting stability and security in the Euro-Atlantic area by protecting U.S. interests and those of its coalition partners.

Furthermore, the U.S. wants to offset Russian sway in Eastern Europe, and it sees this as an important strategic need. By defending Ukraine, the United States aims to reduce Moscow's ability to control its neighbors and limit the freedom of these countries to choose their own political relationships and forms of government. There is also the US' economic stake in the region, such as trade and investment opportunities, energy diversification efforts, and reduced dependence on Russian resources. More than strictly a material interest, the U.S. remains invested in supporting democratic values and good governance in Ukraine, which it views as a strategic partner and bastion of resistance against authoritarianism (Dueck 2006). Strengthening of the protection and promotion of human rights, as well as support for civil society organizations, also demonstrates U.S. commitment to universal freedoms and democratic values. Meanwhile, the overlapping of these various interests emphasizes the facetiousness of US involvement in the Ukraine conflict and even more complex complicity between geopolitical, economic, and ideological factors.

Diplomatic Moves: Playing Nice With European Allies and NATO

The Ukraine crisis has been a sobering experience for the United States on what role is backed up by Europe and its security alliance with NATO. As the events of the crisis continued to play out, it became increasingly important for the United States to develop a coherent and resolute response from our European partners that reflected their role in promoting regional security and stability. This section considers the strategic diplomatic actions pursued by the U.S. administration as it seeks to solicit support, strengthen alliances, and cooperate on responses to implications of this conflict.

As the crisis broke, Washington redoubled its diplomatic outreach to critical European leaders and NATO officials to emphasize that we have a common interest in defending international norms and a rules-based order. These efforts had also been made to form a consensus about the seriousness of the situation and stress the need for joint action to prevent any further aggression so as to take a collective position against destabilizing actions of external players. In addition, the U.S. used its NATO influence to push for a coordinated response to the Ukraine crisis on the basis of NATO's regional security and defense cooperation mission (Sestanovich 2014).

By facilitating diplomatic outreach, the U.S. worked to mobilize European and NATO attitudes and resources and coordinate policy responses to strengthen Ukraine's response capacity while minimizing the risks of spillover effects. Diplomatic efforts were also enhanced through consultations, strategic dialogues, and top-level summits aiming at increasing cooperation in the diplomatic, economic, and security fields. " These activities reconfirmed the Alliance's commitment to European security and served both to build a common approach, which would best deter destabilizing actions, and to strengthen the principled position of the international community. As the diplomatic chess game played out, the U.S. employed a range of tools, which combined skilled negotiations, positive persuasion, and conscious coalition creation to preserve its own unity and multiply collective leverage in the course of the crisis. Through its interaction with European partners and NATO, the United States sought to develop a strong and unified response that signalled resolve, built trust, sent a clear message of deterrence, and underscored the importance of diplomatic unity in ensuring stability in the region vital to allied security.

Economic Measures: Sanctions, Aid, and Financial Leverage

Amid the complex geopolitics of the Ukraine crisis, economic policies have developed as key tools in driving and reinforcing Washington's strategic calculus. The use of sanctions, targeted aid, and financial pressure has been critical in showing commitment to the cause, putting pressure where it's due, and warning other actors of the retaliation they could face. In a mix of diplomacy and economic pressure, the U.S. has tried to manage the conflict and keep the larger region from falling apart.

Sanctions that have been so well scoped as to affect critical parts of the Russian economy are a reminder from our international community that they do not tolerate these types of destabilizing actions and violations of sovereignty. This punishment is an illustration of collective will, raising the costs of aggression and discrediting the economic logic of hostile behavior. At the same time, strategic assistance focused on support for the resilience of frontline states and strengthening democratic practices creates solidarity and endurance in the face of external pressure. This type of help is not just practical assistance, but one that demonstrates that we value the same things and believe in the same principles.

Using financial instruments and interdependence---especially energy-related interactions---as leverage, the United States has aimed to reset risk-reward calculations for all parties, seeking to deter bad behavior while promoting a more healthy form of engagement. In addition, economic instruments of power have been orchestrated as part of a full strategy that combines economic, political, and security factors in shaping enduring deterrence and conflict resolution. But it is important to recognize how the use of economic tools is a precarious act, with unintended consequences and humanitarian realities demanding policy calibration (Yarhi-Milo 2018). The need for precision and caution in the use of economic tools in pursuit of strategic ends reflects an acute awareness of the danger of spillover effects and unintended consequences. And it is here, in the strategic vision of American domestic economic stability and growth that underpins our burgeoning arsenals of global policy innovation, where we must find space for sensible economic action---rather than simply tactical moves with short-term objectives.

Support for the Military: Aid, Training, and Equipment to Strengthen Defense

In the case of Ukraine, military aid has taken on a crucial position in Washington's strategic calculus. The United States, alongside European partners, has supported Ukraine with aid, training, and security initiatives in a bid to build up the Ukrainian armed forces. This multifaceted effort seeks to enhance Ukraine's ability to defend its sovereignty and deter Russian aggression, as well as promote stability in the region.

Military aid comes in the form of general support, non-lethal assistance, etc., which includes everything from advice and defensive equipment to teaching better tactics concerning the effectiveness of units. The provision of sophisticated armaments and hardware and state-of-the-art anti-tank technology constitutes further evidence of our support for Ukraine's defense capacity-building efforts, as well as represents a significant down payment on broader security reforms (Biddle 2004). Specialized training designed to assist the needs of the Ukrainian military is also aimed at boosting professionalism, tactical effectiveness, and cooperation with allied units. By raising the bar on combat readiness overall, these efforts serve to deter would-be opponents while further strengthening defense in Ukraine.

In addition, these cooperative defense measures include joint training exercises, strategic dialogues, and capacity-building to enhance the resilience and readiness of Ukraine's defense institutions. The combined efforts do not only increase the military capabilities but also build up long-term partnerships and cohesiveness in the structure of transatlantic security. With new millennium warfare increasingly taken into the non-traditional realms, where cyber and hybrid threats are to be fought, specific trainings and advisory services in countering these challenges earned special attention. In emphasizing traditional military and cyber defense and asymmetric war capabilities, such initiatives denote an all-of-defense effort in bolstering Ukraine's ability to address a range of security challenges. In the end, amid geopolitical competition, the continued international military aid from the United States and its partners is based on a dogged determination to maintain norms, bolster collective defense, and confront the hard truths of Ukraine's conflict.

Intelligence and Cyber Operations: Spying, Surveillance, and Non-lethal Combat

Nowadays intelligence and cyber operations play a significant role in the conduct of warfare. Espionage and surveillance can play an indispensable role in acquiring actionable intelligence that includes adversary capabilities, intentions, and vulnerabilities. Nations gather this type of information through clandestine means, including SIGINT (signals intelligence), HUMINT (human intelligence), and reconnaissance to provide guidance for their strategic decisions.

Cyberspace has become a critical area for offensive and defensive efforts as well. The game has changed with nation-sponsored cyberattacks, covert penetrations into enemy networks, and sophisticated malware. These virtual battlefields cross conventional geographic lines and create unusual conundrums for world powers. The application of cyber tools as proxies of espionage, sabotage, and influence makes the availability of strong cybersecurity defenses paramount, and our counterintelligence response necessarily vigorous (Mazarr 2019).

In light of these emerging threats, the demand for defense and threat assessment technologies has grown among government and military organizations. The fusion of AI and ML has further augmented the capabilities that intelligence agencies have with their cyber wings. The advent of technology has brought opportunities to be exploited, but contemporary ethics on intelligence and cyber matters are complicated. National security imperatives, privacy rights, and international norms are continuing to dictate the terms of debate in this realm.

The rise of disinformation campaigns, fake news, and coordinated cyber interference shows how powerful narrative shaping and psychological operations are. As a result, managing the public discourse, spreading information, and countering adversarial narratives have increasingly become fundamental components of high politics. The ability to influence by leveraging digital platforms, the use of social media networks, and control over information systems has created new foundations for strategic competition. What is clearly conveyed is that intelligence and cyber operations have evolved beyond the reach of standard kinetic warfare to pose complex problems for which we must find equally advanced solutions in technology, analysis, and ethics.

Propaganda and Media Strategies: Information Warfare and the Control of Narrative

In today's new Us versus Them geopolitics, propaganda is probably the most underappreciated weapon of war in foreign policy. Since the Ukrainian confrontation, then, information war and narrative control have been studied in great detail for their significant influence on events as they developed and responses from around the world. This section investigates the plurality of propaganda and information strategies deployed by several parties involved in that war, reflecting their relations to existing political spheres and new statecraft.

Within this context, it is essential to consider the extent that such strategies intersect with the changing field of digital communication, social media norms, and disinformation distribution. Through a dissection of the programs and strategies used to disseminate certain narratives or distorted images of reality, this analysis will examine how much information warfare has been successful in framing views on Ukraine domestically vs. internationally (Yarhi-Milo 2018). What is more, a consideration of the ethics of propaganda and media strategies can point out the fine line between making use of persuasive communication and exploiting public discourse in the service of geopolitical goals.

State-Sponsored Information Operations and Media Manipulation Boats on the Water As we continue in this section, see if you can discern how propaganda, cyber operations, and media manipulation fit together; their interrelationship paints a picture of influence operations in modern information warfare. Furthermore, the conversations in this edition's segment hope to emphasize the critical importance of strong countermeasures, strategic communication infrastructure, and international cooperation in responding to misinformation campaigns and propaganda dissemination. In the end, the study in this section is intended to bring some light into a dark chamber of how propaganda and media strategies work but also apply beyond Ukraine's conflict as part of an overall model regarding asymmetrical statecraft and the role of information in influencing global perceptions.

Challenges and Critiques: Treading the Line between Escalation and Diplomacy

The search for this fine line between the balancing act of escalation versus diplomacy in response to Ukraine is a multilayered task and topic for critical inquiry. The balance between international feistiness and saber-rattling on the one hand and strategic restraint forces a subtle mix of different domestic and foreign policy factors to be taken into account, with skillful judgment or tactical play. Furthermore, the specter of unintended consequences and unanticipated escalation is ever-present and requires a delicate touch. The interplay between military brinkmanship, economic coercion, and information warfare is complicating the task of managing this half-war.

The need to deter that aggression but avoid all-out war demands a calculus, which factors in the risk of overreach and miscalculation. At the same time, aggressive diplomacy aimed at peace-making has its own difficulties and criticisms. Doubts about the potential for diplomacy in a context of entrenched geopolitical rivalries and an ever-changing world endure. Moreover, the proclivity for diplomacy to be interpreted as weakness or capitulation on the part of hostile parties illustrates just how delicate a balancing act promoting peaceful negotiations entails (Van Evera 1997). The interests and priorities of parties involved create another layer of complication, since there are different goals depending on the group, and past grievances often preclude meaningful discussions or settlements.

The implications of hybrid warfare make even more challenging the complexities of escalation and diplomacy. The blending of traditional military with non-traditional asymmetric strategies diffuses the line between conventional conflict and peace further. To face this hybrid threat and respond in a coherent, resilient manner also requires flexibility that moves beyond traditional models. Yet, detractors argue that when realpolitik is the driving force behind the response and resolve to the Ukraine conflict, diplomacy becomes a farce with neither inclusiveness nor sustainability. Additionally, one can question when the strategic actions cut across ethical and humanitarian imperatives, especially when the human personality of these protracted conflicts is considered. The diplomatic world also deserves scrutiny on transparency, accountability, and fairness in the sharing of tasks among international players.

Basically, there are so many straitjackets and detractions to forge one's way through along the tortuous labyrinth of managing escalation versus diplomacy that requires perspicuity, wisdom, and a relentlessness aimed at protecting broader strategic priorities. To be able to handle these challenges effectively requires pragmatic realism and idealism, grounded on a strong commitment to regional stability and global security. It is in this tangled web that the resources of U.S. statecraft are tested against adversity and the need for discernment as well as principled determination, both in policy conduct and in a range of pragmatic responses.

Impact Analysis: Short-Term Gains vs. Long-Term Regional Stability

The Ukraine crisis and its influence on regional stability and world politics is a complicated topic that needs to be analyzed. In the short run, the war has produced a set of good and bad consequences. US and allied sanctions and diplomatic efforts have done a LOT to undermine Russia's economy and global standing, demonstrating that concerted international action in response to aggressive geopolitical moves really can work. Yet this approach has also aggravated regional geopolitics and further polarized international relations and the security dilemma in the region. And the militarization of the dispute increases risks of inadvertent escalation and miscalculation that would affect global security.

But just as important, and perhaps even more so in the long term, would be the lasting effects of the conflict upon regional stability. Alongside plummeting confidence and relations with the great powers, normalization of annexation as an instrument of statecraft, alongside a general decline in respect for international norms and institutions, all pose deep challenges to the regional balance of power in Eurasia (Gaddis 2005). The cemented political, military, and economic cleavages have left wounds that will not heal except over a prolonged period of continued thanks to all diplomatic initiatives in the world sustained by re-engagement strategies. The effects of the conflict on Eastern Europe's and the post-Soviet space's security architecture are also profound, with possible implications for energy security, NATO expansion, and the viability of non-proliferation efforts.

In conclusion, the implications of the Ukraine war need to be carefully assessed in a broader perspective that goes beyond wins and losses on a short-term basis but looks at long-lasting effects on global security, regional stability, and the future direction of international relations.

Tactical Effects: Assessing Success and Future Implications

Even as we consider the strategic effects of US participation in Ukraine, though, it makes sense to put immediate wins within a broader context of regional stability and global girding. When considering whether these efforts have been successful, it is important to measure the concrete benefits of both diplomatic and military responses---such as Ukraine's fortified resilience against Russian aggression and transatlantic unity in standing up to Kremlin expansionism. And also the large impact of information warfare and propaganda methods has to be considered when tactical victories are evaluated.

But equally important is to recognize the long-term consequences of what America has done in Ukraine. A lingering military armament in the region and continued regional geopoliticization remain challenges to lasting stability and peaceful settlement. Economic sanctions and their impact on the European energy market are fallout-intensive, especially with respect to the viability of transatlantic cooperation.

Instead, the long-term consequences of U.S. actions in Ukraine must be analyzed more carefully. The durability of the deterrent, whether meaningful diplomacy to resolve the conflict is possible, and larger questions for U.S.-Russia relations loom (Silove 2018). Moreover, with the advancement of new technologies, the importance of cyber operations and information warfare in global security architecture should not be understated.

To appreciate the strategic implications of American involvement in the Ukrainian ruckus, one must be able to see past mere short-term gains and factor in long-term effects. This assessment won't just help shape future policy; it will also advance our understanding of the complex tapestry of power, diplomacy, and geopolitics in the 21st century.

***

Biddle, Stephen. 2004. *Military Power: Explaining Victory and Defeat in Modern Battle*. Princeton, NJ: Princeton University Press.

Brands, Hal. 2022. *The Twilight Struggle: What the Cold War Teaches Us about Great-Power Rivalry Today*. New Haven, CT: Yale University Press.

Dueck, Colin. 2006. *Reluctant Crusaders: Power, Culture, and Change in American Grand Strategy*. Princeton, NJ: Princeton University Press.

Gaddis, John Lewis. 2005. *Strategies of Containment: A Critical Appraisal of American National Security Policy during the Cold War*. Revised and Expanded ed. New York:

Oxford University Press.

Mazarr, Michael J. 2019. *The Folly of Arms Control: Why Peace Requires a New Strategy*. New York: PublicAffairs.

Porter, Patrick. 2020. *The False Promise of Liberal Order: Nostalgia, Delusion, and the Rise of Trump*. Cambridge: Polity Press.

Sestanovich, Stephen. 2014. *Maximalist: America in the World from Truman to Obama*. New York: Alfred A. Knopf.

Silove, Nina. 2018. "Beyond the Buzzword: The Three Meanings of 'Grand Strategy.'" *Security Studies* 27 (1): 27–57.

Van Evera, Stephen. 1997. *Guide to Methods for Students of Political Science*. Ithaca, NY: Cornell University Press.

Yarhi-Milo, Keren. 2018. *Who Fights for Reputation: The Psychology of Leaders in International Conflict*. Princeton, NJ: Princeton University Press.

4
Enabling Kyiv
U.S. Support, Alliance Dynamics, and European Burdens

History and Origins of U.S. Involvement

Global power play, regional geopolitics, and historical connections intricately weave the backdrop of U.S. intervention in Ukraine. American interest in Ukraine began with the collapse of the Soviet Union and the birth of an independent Ukraine in 1991. Being one of the largest and most significant former Soviet republics, Ukraine's geopolitical significance was obvious to leading global powers, especially the US. The geopolitics of Ukraine has its own unique history and culture. Throughout history Ukraine has been a cultural crossroads with numerous people, empires, and civilizations living here or invading it. Aid to Ukraine is ultimately a cause aimed at assisting the people of Ukraine in achieving their aspirations for democracy, sovereignty, and independence.

The 2004 Orange Revolution, which saw power transferred peacefully and promised democratic reforms, buttressed the story that Ukraine was a nation of Western values (Dueck 2006). The United States also has deep historical and cultural links in Ukraine, especially with the Ukrainian diaspora; this has nourished a sense of emotional attachment. These connections have significantly impacted U.S. policy toward Ukraine, providing vigorous support for the independence and autonomy of the country at multiple levels of government. Further, the strategic imperatives to promote stability and security in Europe (to prevent a return of hegemonic spheres of influence) have accentuated U.S. support for Ukraine.

As the post-Cold War European security architecture developed, Ukraine's geopolitical location became more and more crucial to both defining the balance of power in the region and establishing regional order (Brands 2022). Accordingly, the historical background and origins of U.S. policy in Ukraine represent an intersection between geopolitical, historical, and normative forces that have helped shape a gamut of interactions not just across the Atlantic but also in the global arena for power.

Means and Ends: Principles of Deterrence and Diplomacy

With the changing geopolitical environment in Eastern Europe, the United States has had to take a mixture of approaches with regard to its strategic interests in the region. "The central task for us is to be neither weak nor reckless, and this is difficult," it is said, as "the scenario in Ukraine covers two degrees of difficulty: you have the war itself, and then you have its regional implications." At the heart of that strategic need are the Russian attacks, their territorial expansion, and the pressure they exert for a peaceful resolution. Such duality points out the difficulties surrounding US interest in the region and the need for a calibrated approach that balances assertiveness with caution.

Deterrence: Keep the Ukrainian military strong to preserve Ukraine's capabilities and readiness.

This aspect does not solely entail the supply of sophisticated arms and equipment but also includes access to thoroughgoing training and tactical support that dovetail with Ukraine's defensive capacity (Biddle 2004). And by deterrence I mean not only to convey to Putin a serious commitment to Ukraine's security but also the more general fact that we still care about international law and territorial sovereignty. At the same time, diplomacy aims to engage in a serious conversation with all actors---including Russia---to identify ways for de-escalation and a peaceful solution. It will take skillful diplomatic footwork, using multilateral fora, and rallying allies and partners to apply diplomatic pressure on Moscow. It also involves continued engagement with the leadership (in Kiev) to assist political and institutional reform, which is ultimately what will bring longer-term stability and resilience. The challenge is to ensure that the two approaches mutually reinforce each other, creating a solid and effective strategic stance. A pragmatic mix of deterrence with diplomacy will require sound policy choices, clear signaling, and a determination to uphold regional collective security. The United States aims to balance seemingly conflicting goals in order to advance its broader European interests.

Military Assistance: Arms, Training, and Tactical Support

The supply of military assistance to Ukraine appeared to have played a key role in the strategy of the US in the region and reflected its willingness to support the Ukrainian army with self-protection. By providing advanced weapons, including anti-tank missiles and counter-artillery radars---as well as other defensive systems---the United States creates conditions where Ukraine can fight back effectively against not just Russian regular troops but also Russian-backed separatists. That aid also includes the most robust training programs to enhance Ukrainian soldier readiness and proficiency, giving them all the skills they need to use that equipment and navigate complex battlefield environments. Beyond equipping and training, the United States provides tactical support to Ukrainian forces---working hand-in-hand with them to analyze changing security conditions and devise operational plans in response.

This cooperation includes information sharing, joint training or planning activities, and advisory assistance to help ensure the effective use of military aid in support of overall defense strategy and to promote greater compatibility between Ukraine's forces and those of other allies. Furthermore, the technical and physical aspects of aid are absolutely key; without the necessary training for technical capacity building, maintenance, repair, and logistics support, destroyed hardware can easily become completely worthless trash.

The creation of strong supply chains, as well as the assistance in updating equipment, is evidence of the seriousness and intensity of U.S. commitment to strengthening Ukraine's defense capability---guaranteeing its resistance to external pressures and readiness for hostilities. Fundamentally, the military aid package mirrors the multi-faceted policy that the U.S. has taken to enhance Ukraine's defense capabilities---focusing on the synchronization of substantial support, capacity building, and strategic cooperation.

The US priority to help create a strong and self-sufficient Ukrainian military serves the broader purpose of enhancing stability in Europe, including collective deterrence, by sending an unequivocal message of resolve and alliance unity amid a highly uncertain geopolitical environment under hostile strategic provocations.

Alliance Coherence: NATO Dynamics in the Ukrainian Theater

NATO's Ukraine play is an important facet of the larger geopolitical environment and shows its ability to deal with regional issues while, at the same time, holding a strategic course. In this sense, some analysts have paid much attention to NATO's cohesion and collective response after Russia's annexation of Crimea and continuous intervention in Eastern Ukraine. The alliance's position on these developments indicates the complicated relationship between deterrence, dialogue, and disapproval that underpins its strategic stance. And the affordability of a united NATO stance vis-à-vis Ukraine is a major parameter of European security arrangements. For participating states grappling with difficult political calculations and historical sensitivities, building and maintaining alliance unity becomes crucial in solidifying a credible and forceful response (Sestanovich 2014). Regular reexamination of the role of NATO in response to changing security threats is necessary as a sign of firmness and deterrence. Accordingly, a deeper understanding of NATO's internal dynamics in the Ukrainian 'theater' is essential for understanding the alliance's adaptability, consensus-generating processes, and willingness to ensure European-Atlantic stability.

Economic Assistance and Sanctions Regimes

Economic help and establishment of the sanctions regimes represent critical components in the United States' broader geopolitical policy to maintain stability, promote diplomacy, and retaliate against acts of aggression that occur in Ukrainian space. In addition to overall assistance, economic aid reinforces Ukraine's financial stability, assists with sustainable development, and deals with the socio-economic effects of the conflict. And in addition, this work is tightly coupled with the preservation of a sustained sanctions trajectory that would have a two-fold impact on our adversaries---putting pressure on them and rewarding others to follow international norms. The sanctions packages are carefully calibrated with our European partners and other allies to ratchet up the pressure, deter further aggression, and show unshakeable support for Ukraine's territorial integrity (Yarhi-Milo 2018). It is believed that using economic tools in conjunction with military support and diplomacy is a comprehensive approach that acknowledges the multilateral nature of this situation.

However, navigating this delicate balance between punitive measures and their potential impact on global trade, energy dynamics, and regional stability, particularly with the assistance of allies like France, requires careful consideration of the potential backlash from a robust response. This balancing act requires strong and savvy leadership, coordination with European partners, and a watchful eye regarding the effectiveness of the sanctions regime, including its unintended consequences, ensuring that any negative effects on innocent populations are minimized while maintaining pressure for desired strategic ends. The economic component of aid and sanctions shows how diplomatic, security, and economic initiatives are interlinked and reiterates the necessity for an integrated approach to facing aggression in defense of democratic principles. In this difficult environment, the next chapter explores the changing calculus facing European allies as they consider their roles in sharing the burden of supporting Ukraine and make strategic adjustments in light of the continuing crisis.

European Allies: Burden Sharing and Strategic Realignments

European allies are vital to the context of burden sharing and strategic shifts for political contingencies. The transatlantic relationship, especially in the context of NATO, is the most important part of our cooperation on defense and security. As the United States continues to provide military and economic assistance to Ukraine, evaluating what European allies are doing---and should do---to deter aggression and buttress international norms is increasingly crucial. As outwardly expressed in NATO itself, burden-sharing doesn't cover only financial burdens. As much attention as we may devote to defense funding, we should also examine the deployment of troops, capabilities, and arms to maintain regional security. Strategic realignments require a new look at force posture, operational capabilities, and interoperability with allied countries.

The EU's partners are adapting their military doctrines and joint exercises to ensure our common security, in response to evolving threats and in support of common values. In addition, burden sharing encompasses wider resilience and hybrid warfare capacity areas. Investments in cybersecurity, the sharing of intelligence, and counterterrorism measures are the essence of collective security. Through building an all-in, whole-of-government approach to deterrence, European allies are strengthening the overall posture of deterrence against adversarial actors as well as their readiness for confronting multiple threats.

The shifts, evident in the strategic realignments occurring in the European theater, have to be balanced out, given regional geopolitical context and threat perception. Across Baltic and Black Sea nations, the fine-tuning of defense postures has emphasized a joint reaction to assertiveness in nearby territories. By adopting a forward policy, allied troops would demonstrate their determination to defend the territory of nation-states and stabilize the east. Negotiating the intricate dance of burden sharing and strategic recalibration involves diplomatic bargaining, policy coordination, and alliance policy consensus. It necessitates a nuanced balancing of national interests and the security of all parties, all of which are integral to the overarching goal of maintaining peace and stability (Porter 2020). Thus the ongoing debate and decision-making within NATO illustrates the continuing importance of European allies in crafting game changers in biopolitics and global geopolitics.

Public Opinion and Geopolitical Legitimacy

Public perception and legitimacy in geopolitics are essential components for influencing conditions of international relations. The public opinion of Americans and Europeans largely influences international leaders' strategic decisions regarding the United States' support of Ukraine. How one views the Ukrainian conflict, the moral case for intervention, and where it intersects with national interests reveals everything about who is making those efforts to keep public opinion in line.

Geopolitical legitimacy: the recognition of authority and right in international relations is also critical. To garner international support, a legitimate geopolitical narrative is needed that opposes Russia's aggressiveness and supports Ukraine (Dueck 2006). Here, we examine the dynamics between popular opinion and geopolitical legitimacy and their effects on U.S. behavior towards Ukraine. We look at the way in which policymakers struggle to frame public opinion and lay down the foundations of legitimacy for their policies, not least when confronted with a complex international landscape. We also probe the influence of media, discourse, and activism on public opinion formation and its importance to overall strategy. We also analyze the significance of establishing and maintaining geostrategic legitimacy among the wider international community. That means bringing U.S. support for Ukraine in line with well-recognized principles of international law, human rights, and security norms. We also consider how attitudes and geopolitical legitimacy influence alliance dynamics in two ways, pressing cohesion and the commitment of European allies to support Ukraine. Finally, we provide an insight into the nuances involved in maintaining a balanced approach between the popular sentiment and geopolitical necessity, arguing that transparency, ethical leadership, and strategic communication are indispensable for gaining public trust and geopolitical legitimacy in the face of formidable challenges.

Russian countermoves: Regional Implications

Russia's reaction to U.S. backing for Ukraine has been several-fold and reflects its strategic imperatives and stakes in the region. Moscow's responses have been a mix of military, diplomatic, and economic actions calculated to strengthen its position while at the same time making clear that charging into what it regards as its backyard comes with costs. In terms of hard power, Russia has stepped up its military presence and capabilities along its western borders, holding extensive military exercises, upgrading its armed forces, and deploying high-tech weapons to Crimea and other key regions near Ukraine. This more assertive stance is both a show of strength and a sign of Moscow's readiness to react forcefully to perceived challenges from Ukraine, as well as the broader Euro-Atlantic alliance. In diplomatic terms, Moscow has tried to divide the West by identifying cleavages among Western powers and within NATO and the

European Union, calling into question claims of their support for Ukraine, and driving a wedge between allied nations. Gilad Erdan, the Israeli minister of strategic affairs and public diplomacy, said in a statement (in **January 2019**,) that contacts with states like Ukraine should take place "without preconditions." In addition, Moscow has pursued an aggressive diplomatic effort toward countries in Eastern Europe and Central Asia---working to cultivate closer ties and weaken Western influence in some key areas. Economically, Russia has turned energy and financial inducements into sources of influence by using its position as Europe's top supplier of natural gas to offer cash-starved governments financing while encouraging pro-Russian sentiment in an effort to undermine Western sanctions. They are the product of Russian resolve to secure strategic rear areas and assert itself within this region in ways that seriously complicate the longstanding commitment of Western powers, including but not limited to the United States and its partners, to support Ukraine and to push back against Russian aggression. The ripple effects of Russia's moves against Ukraine can be felt not just in the immediate Ukraine theater but across the larger geopolitical landscape of Eastern Europe---where erstwhile empires met crushed dreams and fascism was born---where geopolitical fault lines and ipso facto sovereignties vie for control. The region's tapestry of alliances, dependencies, and historical memories leaves it vulnerable to possible escalations or struggles for power that could upset the fragile balance that has endured since the end of the Cold War (Gaddis 2005). Indeed, European security cannot be secured by the endeavors of regional actors alone---and this includes security implications of Russia's malfeasances---let alone a larger Euro-Atlantic space.

Challenges to Sustained Support: Domestic and International Factors

On both domestic and international fronts, the US' continued support for Ukraine is under attack. Within any country, political transitions carry the risk of shifts in foreign policy preferences and associated budget allocations, such that Ukraine also might experience changes in levels of external support. In addition, public opinion and media attention may increasingly shape perceptions of Ukraine's importance in the wider U.S. strategic sense. International support for Ukraine becomes increasingly challenging due to geopolitical realities and the policies of other powers abroad. Competing interests, such as conflicts in other parts of the world or global economic downturns, can also divert attention from Ukraine, despite its proximity. Moreover, the tangled global network of alliances and partnerships could impose conflicting demands on U.S. diplomatic and military resources, leading to a precarious division of engagement in multiple theaters. Adding to all this is the ever-shifting scene of war, which itself presents a difficult array. The support backdrop must remain under constant review, and the dynamics in the region, of strategy & tactics & all players' intentions, warrant continuous calibrating.

The prospect of escalation and the molding objective of bringing about a stable peace in the region add to the complications surrounding the continued aid policy. There are also economic calculations playing out, with competitive trade interests and energy dependencies on the part of major players muddled together with strategic posturing in Ukraine. We need to step back and consider how our sanctions regimes are affecting the global economy in a sustainable way that would ensure ongoing support for Ukraine (Mazarr 2019)." While addressing these, the challenge is how to comprehend the complexity of the conflict, diplomatic finesse in handling international relationships, and nuancification of mobilizing a domestic audience for sustained engagement. It is a matter of careful calibration, matching strategic imperatives to geopolitical realities---threading the while a web of international relationships and intertwined national (read election) interests.

Long-Term Vision and the Future of US-Ukraine Relations

As we contemplate the future of U.S.-Ukraine relations, we need to remember that a long-range perspective is required, and we have to look beyond immediate challenges and even crises. The enduring relationship between the United States and Ukraine reflects a multi-faceted approach and includes diplomatic and economic security assistance, humanitarian efforts, trade relations, and new investments in Ukraine's independent future. A cornerstone of this long view is maintenance of Ukraine's sovereignty and territorial integrity. The United States needs to reaffirm consistently its commitment to international law and Ukraine's independence against external aggression. The prospect of

U.S.-Ukraine relations is developing a system of institutional cooperation and closer ties between our countries. This includes the development of trade and investment, cultural exchange, and education partnership opportunities. By strengthening these connections, it would be possible to generate mutual understanding and action between the two countries to establish lasting friendship and prosperity.

A further key element of our long-term vision is working towards democratic and governance reform in Ukraine. America can be a critical player to help these efforts for greater transparency, accountability, and rule of law. In so doing, Ukraine will enhance its status as a democratic nation and help stimulate economic growth and social development. When looking into the future of U.S.-Ukraine relations, it's imperative to analyze this strategic partnership in regional and global contexts. By actively participating in multilateral organizations and alliances, the United States and Ukraine could project influence on issues of mutual concern---from security and stability in Eastern Europe to combating global challenges like climate change and cyber threats.

Ultimately, the ever-evolving U.S.-Ukraine Partnership calls for flexibility and foresight. At the same time as the strategic terrain changes, both countries also need to be nimble in their response to new threats and opportunities. This requires continual conversation and periodic check-ins on shared priorities and the ability to pivot when conditions demand it. In the end, the future of U.S.-Ukraine relations depends on a stable long-term policy that consists of principled support, comprehensive cooperation, and strategic flexibility (Silove 2018). By embracing this vision, the United States strengthens its partnership with Ukraine, helps maintain regional peace, and defends a rules-based global system.

***

Biddle, Stephen. 2004. *Military Power: Explaining Victory and Defeat in Modern Battle*. Princeton, NJ: Princeton University Press.

Brands, Hal. 2022. *The Twilight Struggle: What the Cold War Teaches Us about Great-Power Rivalry Today*. New Haven, CT: Yale University Press.

Dueck, Colin. 2006. *Reluctant Crusaders: Power, Culture, and Change in American Grand Strategy*. Princeton, NJ: Princeton University Press.

Gaddis, John Lewis. 2005. *Strategies of Containment: A Critical Appraisal of American National Security Policy during the Cold War*. Revised and Expanded ed. New York: Oxford University Press.

Mazarr, Michael J. 2019. *The Folly of Arms Control: Why Peace Requires a New Strategy*. New York: PublicAffairs.

Porter, Patrick. 2020. *The False Promise of Liberal Order: Nostalgia, Delusion, and the Rise of Trump*. Cambridge: Polity Press.

Sestanovich, Stephen. 2014. *Maximalist: America in the World from Truman to Obama*. New York: Alfred A. Knopf.

Silove, Nina. 2018. "Beyond the Buzzword: The Three Meanings of 'Grand Strategy.'" *Security Studies* 27 (1): 27–57.

Van Evera, Stephen. 1997. *Guide to Methods for Students of Political Science*. Ithaca, NY: Cornell University Press.

Yarhi-Milo, Keren. 2018. *Who Fights for Reputation: The Psychology of Leaders in International Conflict*. Princeton, NJ: Princeton University Press.

5
Case Study II: East Asia Pivot
Japan, China, and the Indo-Pacific Contest

Background: After the War Partners and Strategic Tilts

After World War II, the United States led a transition in the security game. The San Francisco peace treaty of 1951 officially brought an end to U.S. occupation in Japan and set the stage for Japan's reintegration into a world system increasingly dominated by American power. The post-war security treaty signed by the U.S. and Japan in turn would form a permanent military alliance with Japan as its strategic linchpin of defense in Asia. At the same time, the U.S. was forced to drastically increase its presence in South Korea during the Korean War, ending with the annexation of a Mutual Defense Treaty with South Korea in 1953. This commitment further extended the U.S. security coverage for Korea, and its impact has left a mark on relations in Northeast Asia (Gaddis 2005).

Its deepening ties with Taiwan, the Philippines, and other regional actors also solidified America's involvement in East Asia. Nevertheless, the subsequent normalization of U.S.-China relations in the 1970s---especially through the Shanghai Communique---set off a strategic reorientation that reverberated across Asia. As China has surged economically, rearranging power and influence in the process, alliance structures have changed, and U.S. strategic priorities have required a rethink.

East Asia has always played out strategic considerations

against a backdrop of historical baggage, territorial quarrels, and claims to maritime territories. I The legacy of colonialism and historical conflicts reveals the complex web of relationships between countries in this area. During this transformation, the United States has had to balance its alliances, maintain stability, and mitigate potential conflicts (Brands 2022).

Post-war reconciliations and strategies are still part of East Asia's mindset today. The interface of historical legacies, changing power dynamics, and emerging challenges makes it important to explore the underpinning history behind U.S. alliances in Asia, which reveals why they matter for contemporary strategic thinking.

China's Ascent: Power, Security, and the Future of International Politics

China's meteoric rise in recent decades as a global economic power has adjusted international politics in East Asia and beyond. China, the world's second-largest economy, has used its economic strength to gain more political edge, regionally and globally. The Belt and Road Initiative (BRI)---a massive infrastructure and investment project---showcases the extent to which China wishes to build networks, increase connectivity, and influence other regions through soft power. Second, China's growing influence within international financial institutions is a way for it to try to shape the rules of the global economy.

China's military power has grown along with its economic power. It has gone from being mostly a land-based force to a multi-dimensional force that includes air, sea, and cyber capabilities. The PLA has also undergone reforms, modernized with new tech, and also leaned towards the defense industry to become more self-dependent. Aircraft carriers, stealth warplanes, and hypersonic missiles are three recent examples of China's deepening military reach and technical prowess (Biddle 2004).

Economic Growth and Military Modernization This dual rise of economic and military power has positioned the People's Republic of China in a peculiar conundrum. On the one hand, China's internal ambitions revolve around stability and prosperity. China's military buildup in the South China Sea has alarmed neighboring countries and sparked a discussion about the balance of power in East Asia. The complex and intersecting domains of economics and security complicate the tasks facing policymakers and stakeholders alike, who must carefully manage alliances, trade relationships, and borders, among others.

More importantly, the intertwining forces of economic interdependence and strategic rivalry have highlighted the nuanced nature of Sino-US relations. Economic relations between the two world powers are still vast, but China's trade imbalances, intellectual property policies, and technology transfers have become a growing irritant. At the same time, the Indo-Pacific's geopolitical tussles have increased, with differences being expressed through rising naval drills, military signaling, and diplomatic brinkmanship.

In summary, the emergence of China as a blossoming economic power and a strong military presence has created various implications for regional and international security. Analyzing the nuances of China's (military) expansion while its economy expands and how these two aspects intertwine means everything when it comes to crafting policies that stabilize, building things that cooperate, and fixing stuff before it goes down in the Indo-Pacific.

Japan in the Pivot: Regional Security and Defense Posture

Much like in the case of East Asia, Japan's strategic importance vis-à-vis security dynamics plays a crucial role. Boasting a robust historical setting and economic gravitational pull, as well as sophisticated military capabilities, Japan fits naturally into the Indo-Pacific pivot. The country has been fine-tuning its security and defense strategies to find a way out in the complicated regional situation as it sticks to peace and stability. Even if the country's post-World War II pacifist constitution has (admittedly) its serious limits, it has led to Japan adopting a very nuanced policy regarding regional security. Proactive courting of key allies and a strong defense cooperation capacity have helped Japan readjust in the face of potential threats.

One key to Japan's regional strategy is its alliance with the United States, creating a powerful partnership that constitutes the lynchpin of stability and deterrence in East Asia. This cooperation includes a range involving the joint exercises, intelligence sharing, technology transfer, and mutual defense obligations, which add to the social security structure. The gradual modernization of Japan's Self-Defense Forces, meanwhile, is part of its strategic shift toward enhancing domestic defense capabilities amid an evolving security landscape (Sestanovich 2014). Japan's participation in multilateral arrangements, including ASEAN, the Quad, and other regional mechanisms, epitomizes its pursuit of cooperative security mechanisms.

Tokyo's strategic shifts also complement its economic power, with trade and investment serving as the engines of regional development and interdependence, which would further consolidate Tokyo's reach in soft power projection. It is a difficult tightrope for Japan to walk, heightened as across the divide has been the animosity of unsolved history. These complexities have to be deftly managed, with calibrated military posturing, while continuing the dialogue that could forge a secure architecture for East Asia. As the Indo-Pacific landscape changes, it is clear that Japan's strategic pursuits and policy decisions will reverberate beyond its borders to influence regional power dynamics and strategic resilience.

U.S. Interests and Engagement

The US has been and continues to be not only deeply

but also durably concerned about East Asia, a region that is critical in terms of the international balance of power and economic wealth. Characterized by alliances, trade relations, and security partnerships, the U.S. role in East Asia is an orienting element within its overall foreign policy positioning. Stability, security, and a rules-based international order are fundamental in terms of America's strategic involvement. The forward U.S. Navy presence, anchored by America's major bases in Yokosuka and Sasebo in Japan and naval installations in Guam and Singapore, is a testament to the seriousness of ensuring freedom of navigation and overall maritime security across the Indo-Pacific region.

In addition to military deployments, the United States encourages regional stability through diplomatic engagement such as high-level dialogues with key allies and partners. Economic interests figure prominently in the U.S. East Asia strategy, with an emphasis on fair trade, market access, and investment opportunities. The United States has long supported open and transparent economic relationships, using its influence to construct regional trade architectures that emphasize sustainable development in the Asia-Pacific region. Moreover, the United States aspires to encourage institutional cooperation via multilateral platforms, including the (1) ASEAN Regional Forum and (2) East Asia Summit, in supporting inclusive security architectures and peaceful conflict resolution.

Since then, American soft power programs, including educational exchanges, cultural outreach, and public diplomacy, have helped maintain a positive perception in the region. The United States will adopt a calibrated approach that focuses on deterrence and reassurance, deepening its security commitments while continuing to seek constructive engagement with China as Beijing's growing influence is felt throughout the region (Porter 2020). Through the pursuit of sound and balanced maintenance of its presence and influence in East Asia, the United States becomes a cornerstone for stability in this immediate, volatile geopolitical environment that stretches across the Indo-Pacific.

Dialogues: Bilateral and Multilateral: Promoting Stability

In the complicated geopolitics of East Asia, stability requires lifting bilateral and multilateral relations to a higher level. The region's complex mix of alliances, historical rivalries, and economic ties highlights the importance of careful, thought-out diplomacy. Bilateral engagements like the Camp Treaty with Japan and the alliance with Korea form critical building blocks for regional security and deterrence. Such associations represent long-term commitments and serve as stabilizing elements in a milieu of shifting security dynamics.

Additionally, fostering multilateral engagements at forums such as the Quad (which includes the United States, Japan, India, and Australia) and ASEAN---strengthening cooperation mechanisms for addressing shared concerns. And as they enable the regional powers to engage in dialogue and cooperation, offering a driving force for peace and stability. Ongoing dialogues and negotiations on contested territorial disputes, including in the South China Sea, are also a reminder of the necessity to build stability through diplomacy. The fine line between asserting sovereignty and avoiding escalation illustrates the central importance of bilateral and multilateral diplomacy in shaping regional outcomes.

As the technology changes the nature of security, pillars---like those of cyber security cooperation, maritime partnerships, and efforts to prevent further proliferation---all stand as necessary contributors for cooperating stability. At the same time, joint exercises and intelligence sharing foster interoperability and promote shared security cooperation among allies and partners. These tangible dimensions of bilateral and multilateral relations reaffirm the importance of both for strengthening stability and preventing conflict in East Asia. This is the backdrop that provides a setting for the book's examination of the difficulties and implications of maintaining order through careful, closely scripted bilateral and multilateral relationships in East Asia.

The Complex Interdependence Relationships Between Economic Ties and Trade Policies

As a vital part of the complex system of international relations, economic links and trade policies largely determine the strategic layout. And the Indo-Pacific is no different---intertwined economics between major players ultimately determine their shared destiny, which plays a role in regional geopolitical imbalances. China's rise as a global economic power has meant increasingly large trade and investment flows between China, Japan, the United States, and other regional partners. This economic integration is a force for growth and development, but it also implies various challenges, including those of strategic competition and national security.

The interlocking supply chains, the technology transfer, and the financial connections are the measure of how deep those economic ties are in the region. National leaders will have to tread carefully with those interdependencies, balancing the need for economic cooperation against security issues. Trade issues such as intellectual property rights, market access, and the fairness of trade practices take center stage. Elsewhere, disputes of currency manipulation, export subsidies, and regulatory standards complicate the weave of economic relations among Indo-Pacific countries.

So trade policies, including tariffs, quotas, and free-trade agreements, are also means of influencing the economic dimension for (and of) strategic rivalries. In essence, the Indo-Pacific competition features two visions of economic integration---with contested initiatives such as the Comprehensive and Progressive Agreement for Trans-Pacific Partnership (CPTPP) and Regional Comprehensive Economic Partnership (RCEP) representing competing trade and investment models. They provide a framework undergirding commerce and have implications for the regional distribution of power and the alignment of states on behalf of their interests.

In this nexus of relationships, the United States is looking to reformulate its trade policy in the region by strengthening economic ties while trying to find ways to resolve issues regarding market access and intellectual property protection. At the same time, Japan seeks to use its economic connections to maintain stability and rules-based trade in the region, establishing itself as one of the principal actors driving economic architecture in the Indo-Pacific. While China's BRI signals alternative forms of economic connectivity emerging in the region, regional actors are forced into active consideration of what the long-term consequences of participation in such initiatives might be---both for risks and benefits (Yarhi-Milo 2018).

In general, it takes considerable diplomatic skill and quite forward-policy thinking rationale to weave through this very intricate set of economics used as "a weapon" in security policies. There is a need for active and collective endeavors to maintain a balance that ensures prosperity without creating potential vulnerabilities. As the Indo-Pacific competition matures, the economic aspects of this strategic theater will remain critically important, with deep implications for both regional affairs and for the wider international system.

Security Dilemmas and Risk Management: Peace versus Assertiveness

In East Asia the mixed security dilemmas caused by states' push-pull between peacefulness and assertiveness dominate the perceptional spectrum of the region's complex constellation. It is a region with historical grievances, contested territories, and different security doctrines that makes establishing stability in the region more complex. China's assertive moves in the South China Sea and its military modernization have alarmed countries in the region as well as Washington. Japan, however, has to navigate meeting its security needs in accordance with its pacifist constitution---and when it comes to responding to local provocations. As a major Indo-Pacific country, the United States is dealing with how to maintain a strong security capacity without an arms buildup or culminating in military confrontation.

It is essential to balance deterrence and diplomacy in managing such security dilemmas. Risk reduction takes on a new importance to avoid misinterpretation and inadvertent escalation (Van Evera 1997). Risk assessment and response strategies are further complicated by economic interdependencies, geopolitical rivalries, and technological progress. In addition, the changing face of warfare, such as the cyber and AI aspects of it, poses new dimensions to security problems. Cyberattacks and disinformation for national securities are critical for risk mitigation. In addition, the rise of AI-powered weapons systems has created ethical, legal, and strategic questions that challenge traditional models of security.

The fragile balance of peace and assertiveness needs a comprehensive approach with diplomacy efforts, crisis control arrangements, and an open line of communication. Multilateral discussions and confidence building may help reduce security dilemmas and promote cooperative security structures. However, it is difficult to realize such goals in the face of diverging national interests and historic resentments. Aleppo implications To address security dilemmas involves empathy for others' positions, together with a steadfast commitment to international norms and principles. In conclusion, the delicate balance between peace and firmness in East Asia is calling for careful risk management, sustained dialogue, and common readiness to make regional stability more important than particular unilateral interests.

Technology Advancements and Warfare: Cyber, AI, Innovation

The nature of war is changing rapidly because of the pace of technological innovation, in particular in cyber and AI. In the hyper-connected digital world of today, cyber war has become a pressing weapon in the armory of states and non-states to help further strategic end goals---whether that's spying, sabotage, or creating disinformation campaigns and striking critical infrastructure. With the proliferation of digital technology in national systems, the ramifications of cyber attacks for security are enormous, and hence it is time to revisit our classical defense doctrines (Mazarr 2019).

Opportunities and challenges arising from the introduction of AI in military operations. AI stands to transform command and control mechanisms, precision targeting, and logistics and supply chain management. Yet, ethical aspects of autonomous systems and the dangers stemming from algorithmic decision-making need to be judiciously examined. It is also driving a technological arms race in AI and cyber capability, a period of competitive innovation and adaptation that has increased geopolitical tension.

In this context, it is essential for policymakers and other experts in the defense realm to continue to exchange views with a view towards forming international norms and regulations that minimize risks by leveraging emerging technologies for global security and stability. R&D in defense technology is about more than cyber and AI, however; modernization efforts include everything from quantum computing, space-based capabilities, and unmanned aerial vehicles to weapons of the future. These developments provide new opportunities for strategic advantage and asymmetric war that redefine the conventional boundaries of war itself.

Where technology and warfare meet highlights the need for an inclusive investigation into what these developments mean, how they are being used, and the limits to their scope. Finally, there is a need to encourage greater cooperation between public and private sectors, as well as among countries at the international level, in order to meet the many problems raised by new technologies of warfare. By appreciating the changing interplay of cyber, AI, and innovation within the national security and strategic competition landscape, leaders can navigate today's complexity in warfare and create a future that is more secure and resilient.

How the Region Is Responding: South Korea, Asia, and Beyond

East Asian geopolitics provokes varied reactions from nations in the region and beyond. South Korea, for its part, a key player in the mix, needs to navigate between close economic relations with China and long-standing security ties with the United States. Delicate diplomacy The placement in Korea of advanced U.S. missile defense systems that has caused the powerful China to retaliate with diplomatic tensions running high effects a tough challenge for Seoul's delicate diplomacy (Dueck 2006). Meanwhile, ASEAN is being forced to manage its own complicated responses as it attempts to maintain its policy of non-interference while also navigating the regional military powers with nuance and caution in order to ensure some degree of regional stability. As a highly differentiated organization, including members with different alignments and priorities, these dynamics make it difficult to fashion a collective response to the Indo-Pacific competition.

In addition to these central figures, neighboring nations also are developing their responses. From bold policies in the South China Sea to deeper economic integration courtesy of Beijing's massive Belt and Road Initiative, countries such as Vietnam, the Philippines, and Malaysia are adjusting their foreign policy calculus against the shifting calculus of power. India, Australia, and other new regional players are reimagining their roles in the Indo-Pacific theater. India wants to bolster its strategic presence through such moves as the Quad---which also includes the U.S., Japan, and Australia and seeks a counterweight to China's influence in the Indian Ocean. So is Australia---torn between keeping its crucial alliance with the U.S. and nurturing economic relations with China.

Such multifaceted regional reactions reflect the complex interplay of diplomatic maneuvers, economic entanglement, and security calculations that frame East Asia's scene in these increasingly turbulent times. This delicate balance of national interest and regional stability is a current point of anxiety for policymakers and strategic thinkers throughout the Indo-Pacific region.

Prospects: Challenges and Opportunities for Strategic Equilibrium

With our eyes set on the future landscape of strategic balance in the Indo-Pacific region, we've got to understand all these layers of challenges history has thrown at us---and at others. The world geopolitical situation is changing, and the strategic equation for the next few decades can be quite complex. One of the paramount challenges, therefore, is in managing the increasing rivalry between great powers, especially the US and China, as they endeavor to assert influence without actually coming into direct conflict (Silove 2018).

In addition, rapid advances in technologies such as artificial intelligence (AI), cyber weapons, and space-based platforms will revolutionize the nature of war and the region's security. This technological race presents a new level of risk and opportunity, requiring increasing scrutiny of conventional approaches to defense and deterrence.

Economy-wise, the interconnected nature of world trade and complex supply chains makes constructions about at least managing economic uncertainties and minimizing damage from tit-for-tat trade frictions something that's going to be very closely followed. As regional economies grapple with these challenges, opportunities present themselves for cooperative ventures seeking to promote stability and sustainability.

In this complex situation, the role of regional groupings like the ASEAN and East Asia Summit has become more important in envisaging the future strategic terrain. They offer a space for dialogue, cooperation, and conflict resolution by creating an opportunity for consensus building and mutual understanding among different actors.

Moreover, the rise of non-traditional security challenges such as climate change, pandemics, and transnational crime requires a more comprehensive understanding of security that goes beyond traditional military threats. Meeting these challenges calls for creative policy structures and multidisciplinary cooperation to ensure an integrated approach to prevention and response.

To prepare for the future course of strategic equilibrium in the Indo-Pacific, it is imperative that we all recognize the underlying inter-linkages between the challenges and opportunities. The ever-changing nature of the region calls for flexible thinking and action that adapts to changing geopolitical, technological, and environmental factors. Through a combination of proactive diplomacy, inclusive dialogue, and future-oriented policies, the stakeholders can at least try to manage the complexities and chart a course to balance a secure and prosperous future for not just the Indo-Pacific but beyond.

***

Biddle, Stephen. 2004. *Military Power: Explaining Victory and Defeat in Modern Battle*. Princeton, NJ: Princeton University Press.

Brands, Hal. 2022. *The Twilight Struggle: What the Cold War Teaches Us about Great-Power Rivalry Today*. New Haven, CT: Yale University Press.

Dueck, Colin. 2006. *Reluctant Crusaders: Power, Culture, and Change in American Grand Strategy*. Princeton, NJ: Princeton University Press.

Gaddis, John Lewis. 2005. *Strategies of Containment: A

Critical Appraisal of American National Security Policy during the Cold War*. Revised and Expanded ed. New York: Oxford University Press.

Mazarr, Michael J. 2019. *The Folly of Arms Control: Why Peace Requires a New Strategy*. New York: PublicAffairs.

Porter, Patrick. 2020. *The False Promise of Liberal Order: Nostalgia, Delusion, and the Rise of Trump*. Cambridge: Polity Press.

Sestanovich, Stephen. 2014. *Maximalist: America in the World from Truman to Obama*. New York: Alfred A. Knopf.

Silove, Nina. 2018. "Beyond the Buzzword: The Three Meanings of 'Grand Strategy.'" *Security Studies* 27 (1): 27–57.

Van Evera, Stephen. 1997. *Guide to Methods for Students of Political Science*. Ithaca, NY: Cornell University Press.

Yarhi-Milo, Keren. 2018. *Who Fights for Reputation: The Psychology of Leaders in International Conflict*. Princeton, NJ: Princeton University Press.

6
Geopolitical Dynamics in the South China Sea
U.S. Strategies and Chinese Perceptions of Containment

Introduction to the South China Sea Geopolitical Landscape

Historical Context of the South China Sea Disputes

The South China Sea disputes stem from centuries of maritime activity and competing claims among regional powers. For thousands of years, it has been a vital trade route connecting Northeast Asia with the Western world. China bases its claims on a history dating back to the Western Han Dynasty in the 2nd century BCE, with explorers sailing these waters and establishing a sense of historic ownership over islands and reefs.

Modern conflicts intensified in the 20th century as nationalism rose after colonial rule ended in Southeast Asia. Countries like China, Vietnam, the Philippines, Malaysia, and Brunei developed conflicting views on territory and history. China's "nine-dash line" claims almost the entire sea, reflecting its interpretation of historical connections. However, this clashes with international law, especially the United Nations Convention on the Law of the Sea (UNCLOS), which protects the Exclusive Economic Zones (EEZs) of coastal states.

In 2016, the Permanent Court of Arbitration in The Hague dismissed China's broad historical claims, ruling they lack a legal basis under UNCLOS. Despite this, China continues to assert its claims through military actions and building artificial islands. Outside powers like the United States complicate the situation further. The U.S. does not claim territory but works to preserve freedom of navigation and counters China's maritime moves, while supporting Southeast Asian countries to maintain regional stability.

These overlapping historical claims and geopolitical interests create a complex dispute in one of the world's most strategically important maritime areas. (Kumari, 2024), (Mastro, 2021), and (Das, 2025).

Importance of the Region for Global Trade and Security

The South China Sea plays a vital role in global geopolitics, influencing trade and security worldwide. It serves as a key route for about 21% of global commerce, connecting major markets and supporting economies across the world. Any disruption in these shipping lanes could cause serious economic impacts. The sea also holds approximately 105 billion barrels of oil and 190 trillion cubic feet of natural gas, essential resources for energy stability. Countries like China, Vietnam, and the Philippines seek access to these reserves to secure energy independence and fuel economic growth.

China emphasizes control over areas like the Paracel and Spratly Islands due to their strategic importance. As one of the largest energy consumers, China relies on this route for nearly 80% of its oil imports. Protecting these waters helps safeguard supply lines, boosts its military presence, and strengthens territorial claims.

Security issues add complexity to the region. Overlapping claims create a tense environment prone to conflict. The United States conducts Freedom of Navigation Operations to challenge what it sees as China's excessive maritime claims, supporting Southeast Asian nations contesting China's reach.

Other countries like Japan and India watch the South China Sea closely because of their own trade and security interests. The combined actions of these players create a complex geopolitical web, with partnerships and rivalries that shape international relations today (Cappelletti, 2024), (Kumari, 2024) and (Das, 2025).

Overview of U.S. Foreign Policy in the South China Sea

Historical Evolution of U.S. Involvement

U.S. involvement in the South China Sea began during the Cold War, focusing on containing communist influence, particularly from China. Initially, the U.S. acted to counter Soviet expansion, using military efforts in Vietnam to support this aim. The 1979 establishment of diplomatic relations with China shifted U.S. policy. It balanced Soviet ambitions and opened economic opportunities with China.

As China's economic and military power grew in the late 20th and early 21st centuries, concerns increased about its assertiveness in regional disputes. The Obama administration responded with a "pivot to Asia," increasing military presence and strengthening ties with Japan, India, and Vietnam. This strategy reflected recognition of China's rising influence and aimed to protect U.S. interests in the Western Pacific (Cuong et al., 2024).

Later administrations from both parties adopted a firmer stance. They challenged China's territorial claims in the South China Sea, viewing China as a revisionist power trying to change international rules and expand control over nearby areas (Teixeira, 2019). The U.S. increased freedom of navigation operations and enhanced alliances across Southeast Asia.

U.S. policies have come to focus not only on maintaining stability but also on containing China's rise to preserve American dominance (Teixeira, 2019). Given ongoing disputes over waters and resources, the U.S. will remain a key player influencing regional security and balance.

Key Policies and Initiatives Aimed at Containment

The United States has launched various policies to limit China's influence in the South China Sea, emphasizing its commitment to regional dominance. Central to this effort is the Indo-Pacific Strategy, which builds on the earlier "Pivot to Asia" policy. This strategy strengthens ties with partners like Japan, Australia, and India, mainly through groups like the Quadrilateral Security Dialogue (QUAD) and AUKUS. These alliances aim to balance China's growing military power and uphold a "rules-based order" focused on free navigation and respect for territorial borders.

The U.S. has increased its military presence with "Freedom of Navigation Operations" (FONOPs) that challenge China's broad claims and ensure open sea lanes for global trade. These operations send a clear message to Beijing and regional nations that the U.S. sees navigation rights as a key security issue, which appeals to Southeast Asian countries uneasy about China's assertiveness.

Washington also promotes multilateral diplomacy, working with ASEAN countries to improve maritime security and resource management cooperation. This diplomatic approach strengthens ties and positions the U.S. as a mediator aiming to reduce tensions and encourage peaceful solutions.

Beyond military actions, the U.S. targets China's Belt and Road Initiative (BRI), concerned that it creates dependency on China instead of America. These economic measures seek to limit Beijing's regional sway by exposing and countering coercive practices.

China accuses the U.S. of causing unrest and forcing neighbors to choose sides over cooperative solutions. Coastal states thus face a challenge balancing sovereignty with relationships to both powers.

Overall, the U.S. strategy seeks to restrain China's ambitions in the South China Sea, foster collective security, and assert American leadership in the region. See (Bilal, 2025), (Teixeira, 2019), (Teixeira, 2019), and (Teixeira, 2019).

Chinese Response to U.S. Strategies in the Region

Perception of U.S. Actions as Containment Strategy

Many see the United States' presence in the South China Sea as an effort to counter China's growing power and assertiveness. The U.S. has long viewed China's rise as a challenge to its global standing. Actions such as Freedom of Navigation

Operations (FONOPs) uphold international maritime rules and reinforce America's role against Chinese expansion, especially amid Beijing's disputed claims over much of the South China Sea.

Critics argue that the U.S. stance is hypocritical since it holds no territorial claims but opposes China's claims, labeling them illegal. According to (Teixeira, 2019), some believe these policies aim more to block China's influence than to protect the interests of other nations. This approach risks increasing tensions instead of fostering cooperation or peaceful resolutions.

Experts warn that such containment tactics may backfire by fueling Chinese resentment and complicating U.S. relations with Southeast Asian countries caught in between. The idea that the U.S. seeks regional stability is challenged by those who see its actions as attempts to maintain dominance rather than promote peace or democracy, as noted in (Teixeira, 2019).

China views U.S. moves as unwarranted interference in its sovereign territory. This outlook deepens divisions, shifting focus from diplomacy to military posturing and strong rhetoric, which hinders dialogue and negotiation.

While the U.S. claims to safeguard free navigation and deter aggression, many interpret its strategy as a calculated effort to limit China's global rise, affecting both regional stability and the broader international order.

China's Strategic Objectives in the South China Sea

China's ambitions in the South China Sea stem from its history, economic goals, and security concerns. Central to these ambitions is its claim of sovereignty over much of the area through the Nine-Dash Line, a boundary drawn in the 1940s. This claim asserts China's leading role in the region (Seth, 2024).

Under President Xi Jinping, China has modernized its military and increased its naval presence there. The People's Liberation Army Navy has enhanced capabilities to project power and protect China's interests in these strategic waters. The South China Sea holds vast natural resources like oil and gas, rich fishing grounds, and vital shipping lanes that handle about one-third of world sea trade (Seth, 2024).

China's economic strategy also shapes its posture. The Belt and Road Initiative (BRI), launched in 2013, aims to build infrastructure and strengthen economic ties across Asia and beyond. This effort improves China's access to markets and secures relations with regional countries by offering investments and aid (Ras, 2025). Through these close relations, Beijing seeks to reduce opposition and promote a stable environment aligned with its goals.

China also uses 'cabbage tactics,' layering military, coast guard, and fishing vessels around disputed areas to assert control (Cappelletti, 2024). This approach blocks outside interference and shows China's determination to defend its claims.

In short, China combines historic claims, military build-up, economic initiatives, and tactical maneuvers to establish itself as the dominant power in the South China Sea.

Military Presence and Maneuvering by Both Powers

U.S. Military Operations and Freedom of Navigation Exercises

The United States uses military actions and Freedom of Navigation Operations (FONOPs) to challenge China's broad territorial claims in the South China Sea. These operations uphold international maritime rights and emphasize the principle of free navigation, vital for global trade and security. U.S. naval forces sail ships and fly aircraft through waters China claims, signaling America's commitment to open sea lanes.

As China has grown more assertive, the U.S. has increased FONOP activity, especially during the Trump administration, showing a stronger stance against Beijing's ambitions (Skotsyk & Pokrovskaia, 2025). U.S. destroyers have sailed near China's artificial islands, sometimes nearing clashes with Chinese vessels (Cappelletti, 2024). These missions are not just displays of strength; they help prevent further Chinese military buildup.

FONOPs also reassure regional allies like the Philippines and Vietnam, concerned about China's rising power (Kumari, 2024). The U.S. builds stronger ties through joint military drills, focusing on navigation freedoms and collective security to deter Chinese aggression.

China criticizes these actions as provocations disrupting stability (America, 2002). Chinese officials accuse the U.S. of interfering in sovereign matters. Still, Washington insists these operations are legal under international law and necessary to keep maritime routes free from coercion.

While defending a rules-based order, FONOPs also highlight the broader U.S.-China rivalry, contrasting respect for international norms with efforts to change territorial boundaries unilaterally.

China's Militarization Activities in Disputed Waters

China has increased its military presence in the South China Sea, causing concern among regional neighbors and global powers. Since 2013, it has added more than 3,200 acres of artificial land in the Spratly Islands, building airstrips, radar stations, and missile systems to strengthen its defense (see (Cappelletti, 2024). This expansion supports China's broader goal to enforce claims over maritime zones marked by the disputed Nine-Dash Line.

China uses "cabbage tactics" by surrounding contested areas with layers of fishing boats, coast guard, and military ships. This restricts other countries' access and asserts control, as seen in the 2012 standoff with the Philippines at Scarborough Reef and ongoing tensions near Ayungin Island (Cappelletti, 2024). The constant presence of Chinese vessels sends a physical and psychological message to discourage foreign entry.

Satellite images reveal China's ongoing upgrades on islands like Woody Island, which hosts advanced fighter jets and cruise missile systems. These improvements show China's aim to project power over key sea routes, supported by modern surveillance systems for monitoring the area (Das, 2025). Beijing claims this buildup protects national security and vital shipping lanes (Das, 2025). However, Southeast Asian nations view it as a threat to sovereignty and regional stability.

Diplomatic efforts face challenges because China favors bilateral talks while continuing to expand militarily. This approach raises fears that discussions may legitimize China's claims without leading to fair solutions.

Diplomatic Efforts and Alliances in the Region

Partnerships with Southeast Asian Nations

Southeast Asian countries hold a key position in the South China Sea's complex geopolitical landscape. Their alliances shape the region's response to China's assertiveness and the U.S.' strategic influence. This group includes diverse nations, each with distinct economic connections to China and different stances on its regional ambitions. For example, ASEAN members like Vietnam and the Philippines face direct territorial disputes with China but hesitate to fully support U.S. containment efforts because of strong economic ties to Beijing, as noted in (Kucukdegirmenci, 2023).

Vietnam illustrates a careful balancing act. It enhances its defense through local and global partnerships while maintaining economic relations with China. According to (Cuong et al., 2024), Vietnam has strengthened military ties with the U.S. to counter Chinese actions in disputed waters, but it also pursues diplomatic solutions to resolve conflicts peacefully.

ASEAN plays a crucial role by seeking unity amid outside pressures. However, some members favor a softer approach toward China, while those with direct claims advocate for tougher measures. This division complicates consensus within ASEAN and reflects each country's unique priorities, as explained in (Skotsyk & Pokrovskaia, 2025).

The U.S. attempts to draw ASEAN closer through economic and security programs, countering China's Belt and Road Initiative. Concerns over debt have led some countries to explore alternatives involving Washington. Multilateral security groups like the Quad—comprising the U.S., Japan, India, and Australia—support a free Indo-Pacific and strengthen cooperation with Southeast Asia against potential Chinese assertiveness.

Military alliances remain important, but Southeast Asia must maintain diplomatic ties with both China and the U.S. Vietnam exemplifies this blend of defense alliances and economic engagement, as shown in (Cuong et al., 2024). The region's ability to manage historical disputes, territorial claims, and economic interests will largely shape the peace and stability of this vital maritime area(Cuong et al., 2024).

Regional Organizations and Their Role in Conflict Resolution

Regional groups play a crucial role in reducing tensions in the South China Sea, with ASEAN serving as a key platform. Conflicting claims and China's assertive actions make ASEAN's joint diplomacy essential for promoting dialogue among its members. However, differing national priorities and varied dependence on China limit ASEAN's ability to respond collectively to regional challenges.

For over twenty years, ASEAN has sought to create a Code of Conduct to manage disputes. This effort shows the desire for cooperation but also reveals difficulty in uniting members. Countries like Vietnam and the Philippines favor a firmer approach against China's moves, while others proceed cautiously to protect economic ties with Beijing, illustrating ASEAN's challenge in balancing individual interests with collective action, as discussed in (Bautista, 2024). Whether ASEAN can form a strong united front remains uncertain.

Recently, ASEAN Foreign Ministers stressed peace and restraint amid rising clashes with China. A December 30, 2023 statement emphasized peaceful solutions based on international law, including UNCLOS. These statements may encourage broader dialogue but also reveal ASEAN's struggle to craft effective agreements.

Partnering with external powers increases ASEAN's influence. The U.S. has intensified engagement in Southeast Asia through its Indo-Pacific Strategy to counter China, with alliances like the Quadrilateral Security Dialogue providing security frameworks, as described in (Bilal, 2025). This cooperation strengthens ASEAN's ability to address disputes.

Nevertheless, China's preference for bilateral talks complicates multilateral efforts—a divide-and-rule tactic highlighted in (Cuong et al., 2024). Resource disputes further intensify tensions as countries seek growth while defending claims.

Progress depends on navigating political interests and external pressures. Enhancing ASEAN's internal coordination or partnering more closely with like-minded countries could foster a rules-based order that reduces South China Sea tensions (Cuong et al., 2024).

Economic Dimensions of the South China Sea Conflict

Resource Exploration and Exploitation Issues

The South China Sea is rich in oil, natural gas, and fish, making it vital for countries like China, Vietnam, and the Philippines. Experts estimate the seabed holds about 11 billion barrels of undiscovered oil and nearly 190 trillion cubic feet of natural gas, underlining its importance for energy and economic growth, as noted in (Das, 2025).

Disputes arise mainly from China's "nine-dash line" claim, which covers almost 90% of the sea and conflicts with the exclusive economic zones (EEZs) of Vietnam and the Philippines. These overlapping claims hinder joint resource development and heighten tensions, according to (Dang, 2025). Countries involved have increased their military presence while pursuing diplomatic talks to protect their EEZ rights.

Vietnam is reclaiming land in the Spratly Islands and boosting its military posts, as seen in (Cappelletti, 2024). The Philippines strengthens its hold on Thitu Island for similar reasons. These moves show a strategy focused on defending claims and preparing for possible clashes with China.

China aims to control key shipping routes through the sea, where about a third of the world's maritime traffic passes, worth over $3 trillion annually, as described in (Turker, 2025). Control over the sea reflects national pride, security, and geopolitical competition amid rising nationalism.

Some propose joint resource exploration to reduce conflict. However, past agreements like those between Malaysia and Vietnam have had mixed results due to sovereignty disputes, as explained in (Swaine, 2015). Future progress requires careful negotiation that balances national interests and promotes cooperation.

Impact on Global Trade Routes and Economic Stability

The South China Sea handles over a third of the world's maritime trade, with cargo worth more than $3 trillion passing through annually. This area links major Asian economies with markets in Europe, Africa, and the Americas, supporting global supply chains and economic stability (Turker, 2025).

Tensions have risen due to disputes between the United States and China over territorial claims and maritime rights. The U.S. has increased its Freedom of Navigation Operations (FONOPs) to challenge China's extensive claims, especially those based on the nine-dash line. These actions aim to keep sea lanes open but also highlight the fragile peace in the region (Seth, 2024).

China's military buildup, including artificial islands and stationed forces in disputed zones, threatens both regional stability and global shipping interests. This situation complicates diplomatic relations among countries dependent on these vital trade and energy routes (Kumari, 2024).

If conflicts escalate, shipping companies could face higher insurance costs and longer routes, raising expenses for consumers worldwide. The region's fishing industry also suffers from aggressive Chinese activities, reducing fish populations and causing clashes. Because the South China Sea provides about 12% of the world's fish catch, these tensions endanger local livelihoods and affect larger economic networks.

In summary, instability here risks not only regional players but also the global economy, threatening crucial trade routes essential for international commerce.

Future Scenarios: Possible Outcomes in Geopolitical Dynamics

Escalation vs De-escalation Trends in Regional Tensions

The South China Sea remains a tense zone due to overlapping territorial claims and competing strategic interests. China, its Southeast Asian neighbors like the Philippines, and the United States all vie for control of maritime rights and resources. The U.S. conducts "Freedom of Navigation Operations" (FONOPs) to challenge China's claims and support its regional allies, as explained above. This increases friction and raises the risk of conflict.

Recent clashes between Chinese coastguard ships and Philippine vessels highlight the danger of minor disputes escalating quickly. China's growing military presence amplifies these risks, with encounters becoming more frequent, according to (Turker, 2025). Such incidents could unintentionally trigger wider conflict.

Despite the tension, both Washington and Beijing emphasize dialogue to prevent escalation. The U.S. recognizes that maintaining clear communication channels is essential to avoid accidental conflicts. Ongoing talks aim to strengthen military-to-military contacts, as noted in (Bicker, 2024), showing a shared understanding about controlling provocations.

However, strong strategic interests continue to drive tensions. China insists on its territorial sovereignty and expands influence through initiatives like the Belt and Road, referenced in section 3.2. The U.S. counters these efforts, creating a cycle of action and reaction that hinders lasting peace.

International law, especially UNCLOS principles mentioned in (Bautista, 2024), plays a major role. The U.S. upholds these norms against what it views as China's revisionism, prompting China to respond assertively rather than retreat.

The future of the South China Sea depends on how all parties balance their goals amid U.S.-China rivalry. While talks show some hope, nationalist and strategic pressures make the region's situation unpredictable.

The Role of Multilateralism in Mitigating Conflicts

Multilateralism plays an important role in reducing tensions in the South China Sea, where conflicting national interests create serious risks to regional peace. Rising friction between the U.S. and China makes cooperation among involved countries even more urgent. Alliances like QUAD and AUKUS work to counterbalance China's growing assertiveness and enhance collective security, as noted previously.

Despite these alliances, multilateral diplomacy faces challenges due to divisions within ASEAN. Though ASEAN aims to develop a Code of Conduct with China to manage disputes, progress is slow because member states have different priorities and China remains assertive, according to (Kumari, 2024, pp. 1-5)[3]. ASEAN's unity weakens as some members maintain close economic and security ties with China.

New diplomatic approaches are needed. (Bautista, 2024) suggests existing frameworks are insufficient. Instead, nations should focus on strategic restraint and open dialogue to reshape views on sovereignty and maritime rights. This can help countries like Vietnam, Malaysia, and the Philippines collaborate better with external powers while avoiding escalation.

Joint military exercises involving the U.S., Japan, Australia, and Southeast Asian countries strengthen partnerships and emphasize freedom of navigation, as seen above. These drills improve communication and readiness to prevent misunderstandings.

International law, especially UNCLOS, is key to handling maritime disputes, but enforcing rules remains difficult. China's rejection of arbitration complicates this, as noted in (Kumari, 2024). Multilateral platforms give smaller states a stronger voice against unilateral actions by bigger powers.

External actors like Japan and India increase involvement, turning the South China Sea into a complex arena of influence, according to (Turker, 2025). This complexity highlights the need for inclusive, peaceful multilateral dialogue.

In conclusion, effective multilateralism requires dedication from regional and global partners. Building trust and respecting international law can reduce tensions and manage disputes constructively. Without unified efforts, preventing conflict will be much harder.

Conclusion: Implications for International Relations and Security Policy

The South China Sea is a major hotspot due to U.S.-China rivalry, which shapes security policies and global relations. Disputes over energy and fishing rights cause tension and threaten regional peace. This area is a vital trade route, so any conflict could disrupt economies beyond East Asia.

The U.S. has tried to contain China's growing influence through various policies. However, many Southeast Asian nations view these U.S. moves as unilateral, complicating diplomacy. Critics argue this approach might deepen divisions rather than foster cooperation.

China's military expansion and territorial claims also challenge talks. China seeks economic benefits necessary for regional leadership. This situation calls for rethinking power dynamics and engagement strategies.

Multilateralism is important for managing conflict here, with organizations like ASEAN helping guide disputes and uphold international laws such as UNCLOS. Stronger regional partnerships balance unilateral actions that could increase tensions.

Growing conflicts could reshape global security frameworks, with risks including America shifting focus to Asia and neglecting other regions, as noted in (@ClingendaelInstitute & , 2025). Amid clashing national interests and historical issues (Turker, 2025), there is still hope for cooperation to transform Asia-Pacific relations. Diplomatic efforts and trust-building can improve chances for peace and stability.

Ultimately, navigating this complex situation requires prioritizing cooperation over confrontation while respecting each nation's goals in this crucial maritime zone (Das, 2025).

***

Abdul Rivai Ras. (2025). THE SOUTH CHINA SEA GEOPOLITICAL DYNAMICS AND INDONESIA'S MARITIME SECURITY: A POLITICAL DEFENSE ANALYSIS. https://jurnal.unpad.ac.id/sosiohumaniora/article/download/64461/25870

Nandini Kumari. (2024). THE GEOPOLITICAL DYNAMICS OF THE SOUTH CHINA SEA. https://www.ijnrd.org/papers/IJNRD2411027.pdf

Nguyen Manh Cuong, Kaddour Chelabi, Safia Anjum, Navya Gubbi Sateeshchandra, Svitlana Samoylenko, Kangwa Silwizya and Tran Nghiem. (2024). US-China global competition and dilemma for Vietnam's strategic choices in the South China Sea conflict. https://hsd.ardascience.com/index.php/journal/article/download/550/139/1738

Amb Manju Seth. (2024). Geo political implications of the South China Sea disputes. https://diplomatist.com/2024/09/27/geopoliticalimplicationsofthesouthchinaseadisputes/

Dr. Hasim Turker. (2025). Maritime Chessboard: The Geopolitical Dynamics of the South China Sea. https://www.geopoliticalmonitor.com/maritime-chessboard-the-geopolitical-dynamics-of-the-south-china-sea/

Oriana Skylar Mastro. (2021). How China is bending the rules in the South China

Sea. https://www.lowyinstitute.org/the-interpreter/how-china-bending-rules-south-china-sea

Ankita Das. (2025). Geopolitical Dynamics of South China Sea. https://www.ijirmf.com/wp-content/uploads/IJIRMF202503018-min.pdf

Victor Teixeira. (2019). The United States' China Containment Strategy and the South China Sea Dispute. https://cejiss.org/images/issue_articles/2019-volume-13-issue-3/08-teixera.pdf

Lorenzo Cappelletti. (2024). The South China Sea: A Complex Historical and Geopolitical Landscape. https://pppescp.com/2024/12/09/the-south-china-sea-a-complex-historical-and-geopolitical-landscape/

Oktay Kucukdegirmenci. (2023). U.S. Strategic Containment of China Destined to Fail. https://www.isdp.eu/u-s-strategic-containment-of-china-destined-to-fail/

Dr Lowell Bautista. (2024). Rising Tensions in the South China Sea: The Strategic Calculations at Play. https://www.internationalaffairs.org.au/australianoutlook/rising-tensions-in-the-south-china-sea-the-strategic-calculations-at-play/

Vitaliy Skotsyk and Tatiana Pokrovskaia. (2025). Building Ukraine's Economy Through Regenerative Bioeconomy Interviews. https://www.wgi.world/u-s-containment-of-china-a-unifying-geopolitical-outlier-amid-a-fractured-country/

@ClingendaelInstitute and . (2025). The East and South China Sea Tensions | Clingendael. https://www.clingendael.org/publication/east-and-south-china-sea-tensions

Laura Bicker. (2024). South China Sea tensions force US and Beijing to talk more. https://www.bbc.com/news/articles/cqvvxzv24pqo

Lan Anh Nguyen Dang. (2025). Joint development and China's bargaining strategies in the East and South China Seas. https://www.jiia.or.jp/jic/2025/08/2025-08-05-02.pdf

VOA - Voice of America. (2002). US-China Tensions Rise in South China Sea Dispute. https://learningenglish.voanews.com/a/us-china-tensions-rise-in-south-china-sea-dispute/5502656.html

Michael D. Swaine. (2015). America's Security Role in the South China Sea. https://carnegieendowment.org/posts/2015/07/americas-security-role-in-the-south-china-sea?lang=en Khanzada Bilal. (2025). Geo Strategic Dynamics of the South China Sea. https://issra.pk/insight/2025/geostrategic-dynamics-of-the-south-china-sea/insight.html

7
Proxy Fronts and Strategic Attrition
Mechanisms of Balance-of-Power Politics

Introduction to Proxy Fronts: Conceptual Overview

Proxy brakes have a longstanding importance in shaping the geopolitical scene, as they have always been used as one of the essential tools that powerful elite states need. This section explores the theoretical foundations and relevance of proxy fronts as geopolitical-strategy tools, focusing on their historical background while asserting their beauty in modern international-relations games. At its heart, the concept of proxy fronts entails taking full advantage of such proxies to pursue the strategic interests of great powers. The use of proxies allows states to influence and project power, pursuing their interests on the basis of plausible deniability and strategic ambiguity (Silove 2018). This sinister side of things also allows for the gaming of conflicts and balance-of-power calculations in areas of concern without directly entering into open hostilities that could lead to escalation or more widespread involvement.

Historical context of proxy fronts Understanding historical background helps to explain the complex and multifaceted dynamics of proxy fronts. As we all know, throughout the Cold War, great powers played global power games through proxy wars that employed client states, rebel movements, and other non-state actors as instruments to broaden their spheres of influence, contain enemies, and manipulate regional power relationships (Gaddis 2005). Prominent examples are the Soviet involvement in regional revolution movements and U.S. support for anti-communist groups. As a matter of history, that proxy fronts remain as key elements of statecraft even in the modern era are further reminders.

In addition, with the conceptual introduction of proxy fronts, we need to delve into their operational dynamics and strategic effects. Proxies act as force multipliers and provide states a method to project power and engage in clandestine operations at arm's length, with deniability. They act as spoilers, complicating and escalating existing conflicts or starting fresh ones in the interests of their sponsors. This frequently serves to deepen regional fault lines, feed tensions, and add to strategic attrition as a component of a wider game of balance-of-power politics.

Ultimately, the concept of proxy fronts themselves represents a delicate nexus of geopolitics, strategy, and covert maneuvering that demonstrates their inherent merits as instruments to enable strategic objectives with minimum direct risk. Consequently, grasping these elements is crucial for explaining current geopolitical dynamics and understanding the complex strategies of influence and power projection that are woven through the threads of proxy fronts.

Proxies in the Cold War Balance of Power Game: Historical Context

The Cold War represented a formative era in balance-of-power politics that saw the United States and Soviet Union engaged in strategic competition on multiple fronts around the world (Brands 2022). This competition caused both parties to manipulate third-party entities as proxies in efforts to pursue strategic aims short of open conflict. The concept of this type of warfare was that superpowers would support opposing third-party countries or entities with the objective of pursuing their own interests, but without themselves becoming directly involved in a direct confrontation. The extensive surge of proxy wars had an impact on world stability, affecting the stakes in international and regional relations. For example, in the Korean War communist fighters were directly assisted by the USSR and China, while America supported South Korea. Likewise, in Vietnam the North vs. South conflict was greatly complicated by external superpower involvement. The use of proxies was not limited to armed conflict but also included the economic, political, and ideological spheres in a multi-faceted challenge to the bipolar world order.

The Cold War background both sets the scene and forms an essential backdrop, raising and answering questions as to why proxy fronts continue to figure so prominently today in 21st-century geopolitics. It highlights the strategic thinking of great powers and their use of indirect measures to advance interests---mitigating risks of direct battle. The convoluted and Byzantine historical echoes of these proxy operations persist within contemporary geopolitical formations, reminding us that the Cold War's armature retains a significant presence in our current global order.

Modern Geopolitical Field: Spotting the Proxy Fronts of Today

Amid the complicated world of global politics, today's geographical relationships provide an excellent breeding ground for proxy wars. Today's proxy fronts are a complex skein of vested interests, with regional and global powers competing for influence---and control---through local surrogates. Indeed, the complex nature of 21st-century conflicts and the delicate balancing act that defines their alliance structures, rivalries, and strategic interests make it more difficult to identify these modern-day proxy fronts (Porter 2020).

One useful way of identifying the proxy fronts here and now is to consider where power politics is in flux. Old alliances and enmities have shifted, new allies have been found, and old animosities have been reignited. This has led to the development of proxy wars, in which states and non-state actors fight on behalf of more powerful foreign sponsors.

Moreover, the growth of non-state actors and hybrid war tactics has muddled the distinction between regular and irregular conflict---resulting in a blurry line as to what constitutes direct involvement versus proxy support. In today's world, recognizing new weapons of proxy requires seeing through these hazy lines and glimpsing at those who dictate the motives and players.

The other important dimension to consider when deciphering today's proxy fronts is the ideologically driven trends and clashes. In an echo of the past, ideological schisms have risen to the fore again as drivers of competition, with divergent narratives inflecting proxy dynamics. It is important to understand the ideological context behind these battles: it helps us demarcate the front lines of today's proxy wars.

In addition, the impact of technology and information warfare has reshaped the character of proxy wars in our time. Cyber operations, disinformation campaigns, and economic coercion have increasingly been featured in proxy fights, making it more difficult to identify and analyze contemporary proxy fronts (Mazarr 2019).

A big part of the geopolitical map we are on now, and which ones of today's proxy fronts should be identified with, remains a comprehensive effort combining politics, economy, society, and technology. By unraveling the complex knot of interconnected interests and conflicts, we can learn much about the ever more intricate world of proxy warfare and what it means for global security and order.

Mechanisms of Strategic Attrition: Strategy and Effects

The strategy of attrition is an old concept in the balance-of-power politics used as a tactic to exhaust enemies over time and generate conditions conducive to realizing strategic aims. This chapter examines some of the complex dynamics of strategic attrition and the various strategies and effects that have evolved from it. Strategic attrition at its base requires the gradual sapping of an enemy's strength, determination, and ability to resist and continue a fight. A paramount strategy in this is to use asymmetrical warfare---using unorthodox means to compensate for disparities in power between opposing forces. These could include insurgencies and guerrilla warfare, economic sanctions, as well as cyber operations that aim to sap the opponent's will or ability (Biddle 2004).

Furthermore, the disrupting of supply chains and resource access is another significant component of strategic attrition. The supporters of this approach wish to starve the adversary of these capabilities by impeding crucial supply routes and creating economic hardship. The after-effects of strategic attrition are complex, and its cause creates both a balance of power effect and other layers, with intentioned as well as unintended actions that waive the geopolitical configuration. Though in theory one can imagine a gradual withering away of the adversary's strength that achieves strategic leverage, events in reality do not end up quite so simple. Unintended humanitarian crises, international condemnation, and increased instability in the region could result from long-term attrition campaigns, which will require nuanced risk assessment and risk-mitigating policies.

More broadly, the successful practice of strategic attrition can reshape power relations and thereby also alliances, coalitions, and global perceptions of influence. Consequently, observers and practitioners should approach sustained attritionist campaigns with caution and continue to be mindful of changing geopolitical dynamics. Keeping these caveats in view, a focus on strategic attrition constitutes a differentiated inquiry about power, resources, and resilience in the service of national interests. Through a systematically detailed dissection of the methods and results pertaining to this age-old strategy, both intellectuals and policy-makers are thereby provided with important understandings about the intricacies involved in modern statecraft and the fine-tuning of power in contemporary geopolitics.

Case Studies: Successful Versus Failed Proxy Campaigns

Proxy wars have long been a staple of global geopolitics, frequently instrumentalizing the strategic priorities of major powers. Examples of successful and failed proxy engagements offer valuable lessons on the nuances and consequences of these asymmetrical struggles. There is much to be learned about the causes of the outcomes of proxy conflicts by examining both old and new ones (Sestanovich 2014).

However, proxy warfare can be immensely successful---the Soviet campaign in Afghanistan in the 1980s is a clear example of how a proxy strategy can fulfill key geopolitical goals. On the other hand, unsuccessful proxy involvements---like the American backing of anti-government forces in Syria---show us what an unreliable business it can be, fraught with its own strategic dangers. These case studies illustrate the importance of local dynamics, external backing, and strategic interest overlap as critical among factors that determine whether proxy engagements succeed or fail.

Taking stock of the set of proxy battles across the Middle East and South Asia, it's clear that there are always webbed regional dynamics underlying these clashes. The proxy wars in Yemen, with Saudi Arabia and Iran supporting opposing sides, are testament to how deeply regional powers have become enmeshed in using proxies to further their broader aims. In South Asia too, for decades India and Pakistan have sponsored militants to fight their relentless battle for influence in general and the Kashmir dispute in particular. Explaining these regional dynamics is crucial to understanding the interlocking network of interests and alliances underpinning proxy wars.

It follows that the implications of technological developments for proxy warfare have to be analyzed in detail. Information warfare, cyber operations, and the weaponization of disinformation have become powerful tools in influencing the results of proxy conflicts. The use of such technologies makes these conflicts an order of magnitude different, and attribution and management of escalation are difficult for both state and non-state parties.

In analyzing a series of Argentinean and Persian proxy wars, IZA Factor depicts the case that these asymmetric struggles require nuance in decision-making between strategic necessity and ethical interests. The human cost of proxy wars, particularly civilian suffering and displacement, introduces an important layer of complexity into the analysis. The human toll and the moral implications of proxy wars are critical in fostering informed and sustainable policies in today's increasingly more interconnected world.

Regional Encounters and Examples from the MESA (Middle East and South Asia) Region

The Middle East, and South Asia in particular, are central to the proxy warscape, providing a rich example of interlinked geopolitics and machination. In the Middle East, the proxy wars in Syria, Yemen, and Iraq indicate a complicated trap of alliances, rivalries, and interventions by regional and international players. Not least amongst these complications is the role of historic power brokers such as Saudi Arabia, Iran, and Turkey, as well as that of external powers such as the United States and Russia. Likewise, in South Asia, the historic India-Pakistan rivalry has fought proxy wars in Kashmir and Afghanistan, perpetuating a cycle of conflict-driven competition. These are regional reflections of the complexity of proxy warfare, illustrating its interaction with historical animosities, geopolitical ambitions, and security needs.

Revisiting the regional dynamics It is further only after looking at these regional specifics that the bigger picture of strategic calculus and possibility of escalation becomes clear, thereby signifying the need to place local conflicts within such larger parameters. The secretive and complex nature of proxy wars necessitates a detailed examination of their geopolitical, socio-economic, and military dimensions. Indeed, understanding the regional idiosyncrasies has important implications for those attempting to understand the overall geopolitical environment and provide valuable contributions to policymaking and strategic analysis on both a regional and global level (Van Evera 1997). The interplay of contesting regional and extra-regional interests further illustrates the tangled multidimensionality and spillover implications that demand a holistic strategy for conflict management.

And taking a closer look at the local conditions of these proxy wars in the Middle East and South Asia reveals a spider web of contradictory interests, conflicting alliances, and strategic overreach that can serve as a microcosm for world powers' ongoing struggles. Understanding the complex interplay of these dynamics is essential for developing successful policies to reduce strife, foster stability, and protect critical national and transnational interests.

Proxy Warfare Technologies: Information, Cyber, and Beyond

In light of the current proxy warfare environment, the battlespace has moved from conventional to non-conventional battlefields. Contemporary proxy actors now also exploit a high-tech arsenal to promote their strategic agendas, with the information and cyber domains assuming ever more significance. The influence of disinformation and propaganda to control the narrative and sway public opinion is simply enormous. Belligerents use social media, news agencies, and other mediums to disseminate misinformation or outright lies that help generate confusion and stir discord. Such an information war has now become a key feature of contemporary proxy conflicts, with serious consequences for regional stability and attitudes.

Additionally, the field of cyber warfare has become a powerful instrument used by proxy actors to interfere with, penetrate, or sabotage enemy infrastructure and communication systems. The use of malware, distributed denial-of-service (DDoS) attacks, and state-sponsored hacks are the "underhand tactics" used in this covert domain. Because the cyber environment is so interconnected, countries are actually vulnerable to proxy-led cyber attacks (Mazarr 2019).

Technology-based warfare has taken it beyond traditional arenas of war to bring new aspects to proxy wars. Drones: Unmanned aerial vehicles (UAVs), or drones, have been transformative in their ability to 'see' and apply force from a distance while providing an effective cover for proxies to deliver actions of precision with lower levels of immediate attribution. At the same time, developments in electronic warfare capabilities provide proxy forces with abilities to intercept enemy communications, disable tracking systems, and jam radars---confusing adversaries (and then gaining asymmetric advantage).

The new technological revolution in areas of AI (artificial

intelligence), autonomous systems, and quantum computing is on the horizon and offers great promise for both opportunity and jeopardy. Traditionally, proxy warfare has been more of a theater for human proxy agents to make strategic decisions; however, we are moving into an era in which algorithms and robotics (and even quantum protocols) are our proxies. The accelerating integration of technology and warfare calls for guidelines to control the diffusion and use in proxy engagements of emerging technologies.

As proxy wars proliferate beyond traditional frontiers and norms of military conflict, international institutions, policymakers, and defense establishments are forced to respond and retool to combat the various facets of techno-war. The ethical, legal, and strategic implications of these developments are necessary to inform combined approaches for arising threats and to protect the global security in an information, cyber, and beyond period.

Mitigating Risks: Escalation Control and Diplomatic Pathways

In world geopolitics, with its international proxy conflicts and power jostling, there is a very different balance to be held in relation to risks---one that involves the challenges of both dealing with escalatory control and using diplomatic channels. The dynamic mix of states and non-state actors in proxy warfare can lead to greater levels of tension, which have the potential to risk unforeseen consequences and runaway conflict. So, successful approaches will put escalation management and using diplomatic channels to defuse potential crises first.

It is crucial that analysts pay attention to the dynamics of escalation when it comes to strategic decision-making because it makes it possible for a policymaker to make an assessment of the consequences and respond accordingly instead of simply reacting in ways that are uncontrollable or even blind (Yarhi-Milo 2018). It is these diplomatic pipes that are the lifeblood of de-escalation and resolution, providing opportunities for dialogue, negotiation, and conflict mediation. The offer opportunities to vent and develop common ground to improve the chances of peace rather than violence. The use of established diplomatic practices and institutions like international organizations, multilateral processes, etc., is crucial to handle/provide mission space to resolve proxy conflicts. By a combination of cool diplomacy and shrewd strategy, some areas of mutual interest and common concern can be identified sufficiently to provide the basis for cooperative action in defusing crises and preventing them from developing into full-scale wars.

There are also moral imperatives involved in appealing for peace and non-violence problem solving. The primary consideration in all attempts to calibrate risk should be humanitarian, with an emphasis on protecting civilian populations and avoiding unnecessary suffering as well as preserving minimum human rights in proxy confrontations. In practice, the incorporation of ethical considerations into strategies for escalation reduction and diplomatic engagement helps to build trust, stabilize relationships, and resonate with global norms governing just conduct in international affairs.

In the end, successfully managing these complexities demands a sophisticated appreciation of this tangled web of geopolitical dynamics along with an unwavering commitment to nurturing resilient diplomatic channels and promoting redemptive, morally constructive approaches for preventing and resolving proxy wars.

Ethics and Humanitarian Implications

Moral imperatives and humanitarian implications have significantly influenced the national strategies of proxy warfaring powers and balance-of-power actors. The use of proxy forces for geopolitical goals is one of those issues with complex ethical questions that must be considered through a wide range of lenses. This part highlights the ethical implications involved in the use of proxy fronts for strategic purposes and explores the far-reaching humanitarian consequences arising from these projects.

It is worth beginning with the moral landscape of proxy warfare. Proxies are a mechanism for indirect conflict, one that results in asymmetrical confrontations and thus can present moral problems. These strategies constantly cause the distinction between belligerent and non-belligerent to be blurred, thus risking higher threats against civilian populations of being among those affected by collateral damage. It is accordingly that the "moral obligation" to reduce harm and adhere to principles of proportionality and distinction becomes more central in proxy conflicts.

In addition, great powers' support for and arming of proxy organizations pose grave ethical concerns. That support can create incentive or prolong conflict, fueling human misery and further destabilizing the region (Dueck 2006). Moreover, the ethical issues apply to what proxy actors are doing as well, as they take in skewed loyalties (sometimes one-sided), moral ambiguities, and dilemmas in the context of their conduct.

Humanitarian consequences are just as much a part of the moral geography of proxy warfare. The use of proxies can have broad humanitarian implications such as displacement, civilian casualties, and the destruction of social and economic infrastructure in affected areas. Proliferating men and militarizing women As the dynamics of conflict play out, it is civilian populations in these proxy battlegrounds whose well-being hangs particularly in the balance, highlighting the need for a holistic assessment of the human cost of such strategies.

Pondering upon these morality and humanity aspects are crucial tools to evaluate proxy clashes' wider implications on global peace and societies' welfare. An informed discussion on the ethics and humanitarian implications of proxy warfare is necessary so that policymakers, strategists, and the international community can critically evaluate such policies as a key trade-off. By engaging the knotty ethical dilemmas and acknowledging the humanitarian wreckage involved, stakeholders can work their way toward a better world---away from the immoral brutality of proxy warfare in which suffering for one country's gain trumps all, and towards an internationalism that sees striving to cooperate with humanity's burgeoning patchwork of national identities as burden enough.

Conclusion: Modern Strategy, the Measurement of Effectiveness

Evaluating the utility of contemporary strategy is a challenging task that involves a holistic understanding of the intricate ramifications of geostrategic, technological, and ethical considerations. Assessing the short-term and long-term costs of proxy fighting is critical. Effectiveness can be evaluated not only in terms of short-term successes but also through accomplishments that support broader national or alliance goals (Silove 2018). And we must take into account their effect on civilian populations and the potential for humanitarian disasters when determining whether such modern strategies are indeed working.

Adapting to and shaping rapidly changing geopolitical context evaluation of contemporary strategy depends on it. The fluidity of world politics requires a strategy that is flexible and nimble, capable of adapting to new threats and problems. Consequently, the merit of contemporary strategy is to be judged on its ability to adapt to changing security environments, technologies, and diplomacy and the economic and military means available.

A further important benchmark against which modern strategy can be judged is how much of a descent it represents into ethical normality. With the international community moving towards greater prioritization of humanitarian issues and human rights, moral aspects of military and security approaches have taken on significance. A welcome modern strategy should prioritize international law, human dignity, and efforts not to harm civilians.

Furthermore, the sustainability and long-term stability of a strategy's effects in conflict-ridden areas need to be at the core of evaluations regarding its effectiveness. This requires assessing modern strategies that can also have broader geopolitical consequences, such as those on regional balance of power, alliance solidarity, and unintended escalation. - In the final analysis, an effective contemporary strategy would have to be designed to serve as a force for stability and peace in the world that at the same time protected the national interest and security of parties involved. The strategy needs to convey a combination of messages---a mix of determination and caution, where military forces withdraw while diplomats negotiate, balancing both offensive and defensive actions. Taking an integrated look at these dimensions, policymakers and analysts are able to achieve a better understanding of the total cost-effectiveness of new strategies, modifying them as necessary for challenges in strategic competition.

***

Biddle, Stephen. 2004. *Military Power: Explaining Victory and Defeat in Modern Battle*. Princeton, NJ: Princeton University Press.

Brands, Hal. 2022. *The Twilight Struggle: What the Cold War Teaches Us about Great-Power Rivalry Today*. New Haven, CT: Yale University Press.

Dueck, Colin. 2006. *Reluctant Crusaders: Power, Culture, and Change in American Grand Strategy*. Princeton, NJ: Princeton University Press.

Gaddis, John Lewis. 2005. *Strategies of Containment: A Critical Appraisal of American National Security Policy during the Cold War*. Revised and Expanded ed. New York: Oxford University Press.

Mazarr, Michael J. 2019. *The Folly of Arms Control: Why Peace Requires a New Strategy*. New York: PublicAffairs.

Porter, Patrick. 2020. *The False Promise of Liberal Order: Nostalgia, Delusion, and the Rise of Trump*. Cambridge: Polity Press.

Sestanovich, Stephen. 2014. *Maximalist: America in the World from Truman to Obama*. New York: Alfred A. Knopf.

Silove, Nina. 2018. "Beyond the Buzzword: The Three Meanings of 'Grand Strategy.'" *Security Studies* 27 (1): 27–57.

Van Evera, Stephen. 1997. *Guide to Methods for Students of Political Science*. Ithaca, NY: Cornell University Press.

Yarhi-Milo, Keren. 2018. *Who Fights for Reputation: The Psychology of Leaders in International Conflict*. Princeton, NJ: Princeton University Press.

8
From Containment to 'Lean-Forward'
Historical Evolution of U.S. Strategies

This chapter follows the development of U.S. grand strategy, from the basic framework of containment in the early Cold War through today's "lean-forward" approach. And it examines key historical moments—such as the Truman Doctrine, nuclear deterrence, the Vietnam War, Reagan's rollback strategy, post–Cold War repositioning, and the interventions in Afghanistan and Iraq after 9/11—to show how strategic designs responded to dramatic developments in geopolitics, technology, and new approaches to warfare. The chapter contends that the move toward proactive engagement is a continuation of this quest for balance and, more fundamentally, a search for adaptation between longstanding American national interests and the emerging world order defined by the rise of foreign non-state actors within its transnational space.

The Sources of Containment: Early Cold War Public Culture

After World War II, the United States and the Soviet Union became the world's first superpowers, possessing opposing interests in ideology and society. As tensions mushroomed, containment formed the basis of U.S. foreign policy. This policy, as defined by diplomat George F. Kennan, was necessary to stop the spread of communism, especially in the Soviet Union (Kennan, 1947). There was the underlying belief that it was necessary to prevent communism from spreading and overriding liberal democratic values and international peace.

The institutionalization The Soviet institutionalization of

containment was the result of key efforts. The formation of the North Atlantic Treaty Organization (NATO) in 1949 established a military alliance to deter Soviet aggression against Western Europe. At the same time, the Marshall Plan supplied vital economic aid to help reconstruct Western European countries, encouraging political stability and reducing the appeal of communism (Gaddis, 2005). The Truman Doctrine, which committed US military and economic assistance to countries fighting communist infiltration, consolidated the strategic posture (Truman, 1947). Collectively, these measures formed a complex combination of contingency, ideology, and policy, which shaped the early Cold War strategy.

The implementation of the Truman Doctrine involved NATO and its strategic expansion

The announcements of the Truman Doctrine required specific operational measures. But the institutionalization and post-war security of Europe were all about NATO being the main act. In a world where the free future of Europe was still uncertain, the United States incorporated Western European countries within a transatlantic web and so proved its dedication to working together for security, also consolidating its position as a world power (Gaddis, 2005).

Outside of Europe, the Truman administration formed security pacts in Asia, particularly with Japan and South Korea, thereby extending a global containment strategy across a wider geographical area. This geographical strategy was then complemented with financial aid and diplomatic engagement, thus embodying a master plan that included military compacts as well as commercial and cultural links. However, they also entrenched an ideological split in Europe, creating fault lines that continue to endure. Truman's doctrine was difficult to implement successfully in a rapidly changing world, which underpins the realization about the importance of never resting on one's laurels strategically and has already proven successful in maintaining long-term relationships.

Deterrence Through Nuclear Arms and Mutually Assured Destruction (MAD)

The Cold War led to a nuclear arms race, which changed the U.S. calculus fundamentally. Deterrence theory, which prioritized realization, prioritized the possession of such large stockpiles to deter conventional (rather than atomic) warfare and moved to the forefront. This logic was institutionalized by the doctrine of Mutually Assured Destruction (MAD), according to which neither superpower would take the first step in a nuclear attack or prioritized attack, bearing in mind that assured destructive retaliation would follow (Jervis, 1989). This stable-yet-precarious equilibrium of terror went on to lay the very foundations of American nuclear policy, influencing military posture, diplomatic discussions, and international relations for generations thereafter... escorting a constant calculus of risk into the heart of grand strategy.

Vietnam Era Reckonings: Fault Lines in Containment

The Vietnam War forced a painful, searing re-evaluation of containment. The war laid bare serious problems in U.S. strategy, especially the inadequacies of American military power against resolute guerrilla warfare and ideological mobilization (Record, 1998). The war's gray mobilization, gray moral areas, its human toll, and the home front's divisions sapped public appetite for large military operations and spurred a wholesale rethinking of what America should do—gray—and at what cost—around the world.

Vietnam brought into focus the dangers of strategic overreach and "mission creep," forcing U.S. policymakers to come to terms with the complex relationship between hard power and soft power. This period led to a salutary acknowledgement of the need for greater political sophistication in responding to threats, which resulted in some doctrines emphasizing "creep," "restraint," and "selectivity" in the use of force.

Reagan Reasserts: The Rhetoric and the Reality of Rollback

President Ronald Reagan's administration had signaled an emphasis on a determined departure from containment to a more aggressive "rollback" policy. With its strident anti-communist rhetoric, embodied in the "evil empire" trope, the Reagan doctrine declared an open commitment to contest and reverse Soviet advances worldwide (Reagan,

1983).

This assertive stance was converted into "action" in the form of backing for anti-communist insurgencies in Afghanistan, Central America, and elsewhere and linked to a large military buildup that included the Strategic Defense Initiative (SDI). Ironically, this bellicose policy was implemented alongside direct diplomacy that did lead to arms control agreements such as the INF Treaty (Schweizer, 1994). Reagan's approach thus was two-track, appealing in ideological fervor and defense fervor combined with military pressure designed to take advantage of Soviet economic weaknesses—and pragmatic negotiation. This multi-level offensive helped pave the way for the eventual collapse of the Soviet bloc.

Post-Cold War Recalibrations: Breaking the Mold

The end of the Soviet Union forced a rethinking of U.S. strategy in what was very much an unanticipated unipolar world. Policy-makers had struggled to articulate a new role that would move from containment to commitment and crisis management, as demonstrated by the intervention in the Balkans and Somalia. The expansion of NATO into former Warsaw Pact states was a form of security cooperation unseen before (Mearsheimer, 2001).

But the long-anticipated post-Cold War adjustment was unceremoniously jolted by the terrorist attacks of 11 September 2001. The subsequent Global War on Terror drastically altered U.S. national security preoccupations towards counterterrorism, preventive war, and homeland security, reflecting once again an ongoing strategic debate between active unilateral leadership versus broad multilateral engagement.

Current-Century Transitions: Cold War Mode to Active-Responsiveness

The 21st century saw a transition from reactive to proactive or offensive engagement. The 9/11 attacks were the immediate triggering mechanism for the establishment of preemption as a foundational strategic proposition. This forcible repositioning was facilitated by technological innovations in the three domains of warfare—cyber, drone, and precision strike—that laid bare weaknesses in conventional defense strategies (Kagan 2006, 210).

The strategy of the United States increasingly appreciated the value of integrated, whole-of-government approaches that synchronized anticipated diplomacy, development, and defense. This strategy synchronized defense efforts to address the root causes of instability. The emergence of powerful non-state actors required closer relationships, more sharing, and a new set of capabilities for irregular warfare that stressed adaptability and innovation.

'Lean-Forward' Strategy: Rationale, Background, and Implications

The newest iteration of this evolutionary path, the lean-forward defense strategy, calls for not just a proactive but an aggressive stance to confront problems long before they become crises. It is being exercised to meet the evolving nature of international security, a strategy, and security driven by asymmetric warfare, transnational terrorism, cyber and space threats, and geopolitical competition that spill over classical borders.

That approach emphasizes security and focuses on prevention, deterrence, and rapid-response readiness, which includes targeted strikes, capacity building, and collaborative remedies. It draws its inspiration from the experiences of Afghanistan and Iraq, in which "a reactive large-scale interventionist response was found wanting" (U.S. Department of Defense emphasizes Defence, 2022). The consequences are serious, especially in terms of military operations, diplomacy, and norms of global governance. But it raises persistent moral and strategic concerns about blowback, sovereignty, and the viability of open-ended prow-forward engagement that cry out for delicate balancing.

An Analysis of Serious Military Interventions in Afghanistan and Iraq

The U.S. interventions in Afghanistan and Iraq are crucial exemplars of the dangers, difficulties, and dilemmas of post–Cold War strategic action. Their conduct was defined, under the rubric of counterterrorism and weapons-of-mass-destruction apprehensions, by two operations that degenerated in each case into long-term occupation characterized by insurgency, sectarian conflict, and state-building problems (Packer, 2005).

These operations highlighted the daunting prospect of achieving political aims through military means in multifaceted sociocultural terrains. They tested domestic constituencies, strained international alliances, and global public opinion regarding the legitimacy and effectiveness of unilateral intervention. The cases illustrate the essential importance of nuanced intelligence, realistic objectives, and viable political choices in using force, building force as cautionary lessons for future grand strategy.

Synthesis and Transition: All the Way to a U.S. Strategy for Today

A present-day strategy requires detailed historical insights, set within a broad and flexible context. America has to strike a balance in this multipolar world, one featuring both classic state rivals and diffuse transnational threats. A contemporary strategy thus must stop and successfully apply all instruments of national power—diplomatic, informational, economic, and military—to do so with sustainable international "coalitions" (Mearsheimer, 2001).

At the heart of this task is finding a synthesis between defending our core national interests and advancing democratic values and sustainable global leadership. This approach requires moving away from outdated doctrines like containment, isolationism, and demilitarization, and instead adopting flexible, forward-oriented strategies that leverage our technological advantages and empower the use of cyber options. This entails a critical examination of past interventions that prioritized sustainable and politically inclusive outcomes, rather than pursuing a unilateral approach. emphasized

In the end, successful 21st-century strategy demands a clear strategic vision and domestic renewal through innovation and education, alongside commitment to an adaptive, principled international role. The United States can draw lessons from its own strategic development—guileful and spurious victories as well as harmful mistakes—to create a systematic, adaptive grand strategy for an age of continuity and disruption.

***

Gaddis, John Lewis. 2005. *Strategies of Containment: A Critical Appraisal of American National Security Policy during the Cold War*. Revised and expanded ed. New York: Oxford University Press.

Jervis, Robert. 1989. *The Meaning of the Nuclear Revolution: Statecraft and the Prospect of Armageddon*. Ithaca, NY: Cornell University Press.

Kagan, Frederick W. 2006. *Finding the Target: The Transformation of American Military Policy*. New York: Encounter Books.

Kennan, George F. ("X"). 1947. "The Sources of Soviet Conduct." *Foreign Affairs* 25, no. 4 (July): 566–82.

Mearsheimer, John J. 2001. *The Tragedy of Great Power Politics*. New York: W. W. Norton & Company.

Packer, George. 2005. *The Assassins' Gate: America in Iraq*. New York: Farrar, Straus and Giroux.

Reagan, Ronald. 1983. "Remarks to the National Association of Evangelicals in Orlando, Florida, March 8, 1983." In *Public Papers of the Presidents of the United States: Ronald Reagan, 1983*, 359–64. Washington, DC: Government Printing Office.

Record, Jeffrey. 1998. *The Wrong War: Why We Lost in Vietnam*. Annapolis, MD: Naval Institute Press.

Schweizer, Peter. 1994. *Victory: The Reagan Administration's Secret Strategy That Hastened the Collapse of the Soviet Union*. New York: Atlantic Monthly Press.

Truman, Harry S. 1947. "Address Before a Joint Session of Congress, March 12, 1947." *The American Presidency Project*. Accessed April 3, 2024. https://www.presidency.ucsb.edu/documents/address-before-joint-session-the-congress-recommending-assistance-greece-and-turkey.

U.S. Department of Defense. 2022. *National Defense Strategy of the United States of America*. Washington, DC: U.S. Department of Defense.

9
Ethical and Geopolitical Risks
Escalation, Cohesion, and Moral Challenges

Ethics and the Geopolitical Risk

Ethical concerns are inseparable from the shaping and implementation of geopolitical policies. In international relations, the enduring tension between morality and power is a defining feature, reflected in the contest between national interests and moral imperatives (Nye, 2021). As the global balance of power evolves, determining what constitutes ethical behavior in pursuit of strategic ends becomes a necessary but complex calculation. Moral risk in global politics concerns the possibility that state actions will create ethical predicaments, human suffering, or significant breaches of international norms (Walzer, 2015). This has implications at multiple levels, from the treatment of civilians during armed conflict to the humanitarian impact of economic sanctions on vulnerable populations. The ethical dimension encompasses not only legal statutes but also societal, humanitarian, and historical considerations that inform state conduct.

The geopolitical notion of ethical risk also involves judging the potential for unintended or paradoxical outcomes. Actions perceived as legitimate or necessary in one strategic context may yield unforeseeable negative consequences in another, creating profound ethical and strategic dilemmas (Jervis, 1997). This requires a comprehensive understanding of how risks manifest ethically, including their short- and long-term impacts. Geopolitical actors continuously navigate a precarious slope of ethical trade-offs as they reconcile national necessity, strategic objectives, and global responsibilities. The inherent strain in this balancing act underscores the profound difficulty of moral decision-making in world politics.

Dynamics of Escalation: The Danger of Unintended Consequences

The logic of escalation dynamics is a critical factor in geopolitical decision-making, particularly the risk of unintended consequences spiraling beyond control (Schelling, 1966). The prospect of rapid escalation toward more destructive conflict necessitates careful awareness among policymakers. Escalation processes are often nonlinear and do not follow predictable cause-and-effect models. An initial action or retaliation can trigger unpredictable chains of reaction among multiple actors, significantly increasing the risks of a conflict (Allison and Zelikow, 1999).

An interconnected global system adds layers of complexity to escalation, from cyber warfare to economic coercion. These domains introduce new avenues for miscalculation and unintended conflict expansion (Freedman, 2019). A holistic analysis of escalation must therefore account for psychological dimensions, technological innovations, and the interconnectedness of modern crises. Incorporating de-escalation mechanisms and diplomatic "off-ramps" into strategic planning is essential to mitigate tensions and prevent unintended spirals.

Cohesion under Strain: Alliance Management in High-Stakes Situations

Effective alliance management is a critical component of implementing high-stakes geopolitical decisions. Alliance cohesion, especially in military and security cooperation, is fundamental when confronting challenges with extensive implications (Walt, 2009). In a rapidly changing environment, the resilience of alliance structures during crises requires constant attention. Maintaining unity under pressure demands a multi-dimensional effort spanning diplomatic, military, and economic cooperation.

    The balance of burden-sharing within an alliance must be carefully calibrated to ensure contributions are perceived as fair and to foster a sense of collective investment (Olson and Zeckhauser, 1966). This challenge intensifies during periods of heightened hostility or escalation, where adversaries may seek to exploit apparent divisions. Effective management during such times hinges on astute leadership, transparent communication, and credible demonstrations of commitment to mutual defense (Snyder, 1997). Ultimately, investing in trust, interoperability, and a sustained culture of cooperation is key to building long-term strategic coherence that can withstand acute crises.

Moral Dilemmas: Measuring the Human Cost of Strategic Choices

Confronting the moral aspects of strategic decisions forces an engagement with their potential human cost. Whether considering military action, economic pressure, or diplomatic maneuvers, the essential moral calculus involves weighing strategic objectives against the imperative to prevent death and human degradation (Shue, 2016). Policymakers must balance national interest against humanitarian imperatives, a task complicated by the unique geopolitical, historical, and cultural context of each crisis.

Applying a form of ethical "triage" based on anticipated harm to civilians, infrastructure, and future generations places a heavy burden on decision-makers, requiring a framework that transcends mere strategic advantage (Gross, 2015). Furthermore, navigating the tension between adherence to international law and the demands of practical statecraft is profoundly difficult. Integrating moral imperatives into national security calculus demands a disciplined commitment to principled leadership and ethical governance. This includes establishing concrete policy frameworks and operational rules that prioritize the protection of vulnerable populations (Smith, 2005).

What Role for International Law and Norms in U.S. Strategy?

U.S. strategic calculus is deeply embedded within the framework of international law and norms that regulate state behavior. Respect for international law serves as a cornerstone of ethical conduct and a key source of legitimacy for the pursuit of national interests (Henkin, 1979). The United States has historically played a significant role in shaping these very laws and norms through its participation in treaties, international organizations, and the development of customary law.

Adherence to international norms is also crucial for preserving global stability and fostering cooperative relations. U.S. alignment with established principles strengthens alliances, bolsters deterrence, and reinforces a rules-based order (Finnemore and Sikkink, 1998). In the military realm, international humanitarian law—particularly the principles of distinction, proportionality, and necessity—provides the foundational rules for the conduct of armed conflict, aiming to limit civilian suffering (ICRC, 2005). While the dual imperatives of sovereignty and international commitments can create tension, navigating this balance is a persistent and necessary challenge of statecraft.

Balancing National Interest vs. Global Stability

The tension between promoting national interests and preserving global stability is a perennial challenge for U.S.

strategists (Mearsheimer, 2001). This dilemma requires careful judgment to navigate the competing demands of sovereignty and systemic international well-being, particularly during periods of geopolitical transition.

A key component of this balancing act is evaluating short-term gains against long-term outcomes. Pursuits that offer immediate tactical advantages may undermine the stability required for long-term national security (Ikenberry, 2011). Furthermore, in an era of deep globalization, the defense of national interests is increasingly linked to the maintenance of international stability, as disruptions in one region can have global ripple effects (Keohane and Nye, 2012). Recognizing that national interest now encompasses transnational issues like economic stability and environmental security allows policymakers to better align domestic imperatives with global demands.

History Lessons: Past Strategic Land Mines to Avoid

Historical awareness is an invaluable asset for avoiding the repetitive pitfalls of international statecraft. The annals of history are replete with miscalculations, strategic overreach, and misjudgments that led to unintended escalation and protracted conflict (Howard, 2002). The Peloponnesian War, for instance, stands as an early warning of how unchecked power dynamics and ambition can fuel enduring discord (Thucydides, 1972). The complex alliance system that precipitated World War I remains a sobering lesson on the catastrophic consequences of diplomatic failure and rigid war planning.

The 1962 Cuban Missile Crisis offers critical lessons on

high-stakes brinkmanship and the indispensable role of calibrated diplomacy and crisis communication in averting catastrophe (Allison and Zelikow 1999, 99). More recently, U.S. involvement in Vietnam provides enduring insights into the ethical and strategic quagmires of asymmetric warfare and ambitious nation-building (Logevall, 2012). The 2003 Iraq War, in turn, generated profound moral and geopolitical questions regarding preventive war, intelligence failures, and the long-term consequences of intervention (Ricks, 2006). These episodes collectively underscore the dangers of strategic misjudgment and the enduring relevance of ethical scrutiny in foreign policy.

Policy Recommendations for Ethical Strategic Involvement

To navigate the complex terrain of ethical dilemmas and geopolitical risks, policymakers should adopt frameworks that integrate ethical considerations into strategic priorities. First, U.S. foreign policy should actively pursue a **multilateral approach** that incorporates diverse global perspectives. Consulting with a wide range of international actors enriches the understanding of ethical issues and leads to more robust and sensitive strategies (Haas, 2020).

Second, **human rights and ethical frameworks** must be explicitly incorporated into strategic decision-making processes. Weighing the humanitarian impact of policy options reinforces a commitment to universal values and enhances moral authority (Donnelly, 2013). Implementing structured **ethical risk assessments** for major strategic initiatives can help identify and mitigate potential moral hazards before decisions are finalized (Gutmann and Thompson, 2014).

Third, fostering **transparency and public justification** for strategic engagements builds domestic and international legitimacy. Finally, investing in **ethics training** within military and diplomatic institutions is essential to prepare personnel to navigate the moral challenges they will face in the field (Robinson, 2007). Together, these measures can strengthen the ethical foundations of U.S. strategic behavior.

Case Study Analysis: Ethics of Recent Conflicts

Recent conflicts starkly illustrate the impact of ethical considerations on strategic decision-making (Crawford, 2013). The **Syrian civil war** presented a profound moral dilemma: the obligation to protect civilians clashed with the risks and complexities of intervention in a multi-sided conflict fraught with human rights abuses by all parties (Lynch, 2016). The international response was heavily scrutinized through an ethical lens, particularly regarding chemical weapons use and the plight of refugees.

The **war in Yemen** has highlighted ethical questions surrounding arms sales and military support to combatants, as the devastating humanitarian crisis raised urgent concerns about compliance with international humanitarian law (Sharp, 2018).

Conversely, **Russia's annexation of Crimea** and destabilization of Eastern Ukraine posed a different ethical challenge: how to respond effectively to blatant violations of sovereignty and territorial integrity within a constrained set of options (Mearsheimer, 2014).

Analyzing these cases confirms that ethical reasoning is not peripheral but central to the interpretation and management of modern conflict.

Conclusion: Integrating Moral Obligations and Strategic Interests

Reconciling ethical mandates with strategic aims is a difficult but essential task at the heart of responsible statecraft. It demands a nuanced approach that acknowledges moral principles, international standards, and the realities of power politics (Williams, 2005). As demonstrated throughout this analysis, ethics is indelibly linked to strategic conduct, shaping both the perception and the long-term consequences of state action.

This integration requires a clear-eyed understanding of the trade-offs between near-term expediency and long-term legitimacy (Booth and Wheeler, 2008). It involves a steadfast commitment to international law and norms, recognizing that a reputation for principled action is a strategic asset in building enduring partnerships. Ultimately, embedding ethical reasoning into strategic deliberation—through transparency, accountability, and a commitment to minimizing harm—allows nations to pursue their interests while contributing to a more just and stable world order.

***

Allison, Graham, and Philip Zelikow. 1999. *Essence of Decision: Explaining the Cuban Missile Crisis*. 2nd ed. New York: Longman.

Booth, Ken, and Nicholas J. Wheeler. 2008. *The Security Dilemma: Fear, Cooperation, and Trust in World Politics*. London: Palgrave Macmillan.

Crawford, Neta C. 2013. *Accountability for Killing: Moral Responsibility for Collateral Damage in America's Post-9/11 Wars*. Oxford: Oxford University Press.
Donnelly, Jack. 2013. *Universal Human Rights in Theory and Practice*. 3rd ed. Ithaca, NY: Cornell University Press.
Finnemore, Martha, and Kathryn Sikkink. 1998. "International Norm Dynamics and Political Change." *International Organization* 52 (4): 887–917.
Freedman, Lawrence. 2019. *The Future of War: A History*. New York: PublicAffairs.
Gross, Michael L. 2015. *The Ethics of Insurgency: A Critical Guide to Just Guerrilla Warfare*. Cambridge: Cambridge University Press.
Gutmann, Amy, and Dennis Thompson. 2014. *The Spirit of Compromise: Why Governing Demands It and Campaigning Undermines It*. Princeton, NJ: Princeton University Press.
Haas, Richard N. 2020. *The World: A Brief Introduction*. New York: Penguin Press.
Henkin, Louis. 1979. *How Nations Behave: Law and Foreign Policy*. 2nd ed. New York: Columbia University Press.
Howard, Michael. 2002. *The Invention of Peace and the Reinvention of War*. London: Profile Books.
Ikenberry, G. John. 2011. *Liberal Leviathan: The Origins, Crisis, and Transformation of the American World Order*. Princeton, NJ: Princeton University Press.
International Committee of the Red Cross (ICRC). 2005. *Customary International Humanitarian Law*. Cambridge: Cambridge University Press.
Jervis, Robert. 1997. *System Effects: Complexity in Political and Social Life*. Princeton, NJ: Princeton University Press.
Keohane, Robert O., and Joseph S. Nye. 2012. *Power and Interdependence*. 4th ed. New York: Pearson.

Logevall, Fredrik. 2012. *Embers of War: The Fall of an Empire and the Making of America's Vietnam*. New York: Random House.

Lynch, Marc. 2016. *The New Arab Wars: Uprisings and Anarchy in the Middle East*. New York: PublicAffairs.

Mearsheimer, John J. 2001. *The Tragedy of Great Power Politics*. New York: W. W. Norton & Company.

Mearsheimer, John J. 2014. "Why the Ukraine Crisis Is the West's Fault." *Foreign Affairs* 93 (5): 77–89.

Nye, Joseph S., Jr. 2021. *Do Morals Matter? Presidents and Foreign Policy from FDR to Trump*. Oxford: Oxford University Press.

Olson, Mancur, and Richard Zeckhauser. 1966. "An Economic Theory of Alliances." *The Review of Economics and Statistics* 48 (3): 266–279.

Ricks, Thomas E. 2006. *Fiasco: The American Military Adventure in Iraq*. New York: Penguin Press.

Robinson, Paul. 2007. *Ethics Training and Development in the Military*. Leuven, Belgium: Peeters.

Schelling, Thomas C. 1966. *Arms and Influence*. New Haven, CT: Yale University Press.

Sharp, Jeremy M. 2018. *Yemen: Civil War and Regional Intervention*. Washington, DC: Congressional Research Service.

Shue, Henry. 2016. *Fighting Hurt: Rule and Exception in Torture and War*. Oxford: Oxford University Press.

Smith, Rupert. 2005. *The Utility of Force: The Art of War in the Modern World*. New York: Alfred A. Knopf.

Snyder, Glenn H. 1997. *Alliance Politics*. Ithaca, NY: Cornell University Press.

Thucydides. 1972. *History of the Peloponnesian War*. Translated by Rex Warner. London: Penguin Books.

Walt, Stephen M. 2009. "Alliances in a Unipolar World." *World*

Politics 61 (1): 86–120.

Walzer, Michael. 2015. *Just and Unjust Wars: A Moral Argument with Historical Illustrations.* 5th ed. New York: Basic Books.

Williams, Bernard. 2005. *In the Beginning Was the Deed: Realism and Moralism in Political Argument.* Princeton, NJ: Princeton University Press.

10
Conclusion
Coherence and Danger in America's Hidden Grand Design

A Recap of America's Strategic Journey

The United States' strategic odyssey has not only been an episodic, ever-changing saga, but it has also had direct bearings from historicity to the global calculus of power. Over the years as a global leader, the U.S. has worked through different strategic frameworks to respond to threats and opportunities as they arise yet preserve its role as a dominant player in world events. The early Cold War years saw the crystallization of containment as a central guiding principle centered on the limitation (and rollback—or de-Stalinization) of communism and the maintenance of Western influence. The second way was that of alliances such as NATO and SEATO, both of which demonstrated the U.S.'s resolve to collective security and democratic principles.

The sudden dissolution of the Soviet Union heralded a new era in which American strategic priorities would be reconsidered. The post-Cold War was one in which the world was a unipolar world, something that the form of policies like the expansion of NATO or even spreading liberal democracy would suggest exists. However, 9/11 caused a tectonic shift in America's strategic priorities—counterterrorism rose to the top. The Global War on Terror became the prism for U.S. national security: military interventions, foreign aid, and intelligence efforts were viewed through its lens. At the same time, however, a rising China and a resurgent Russia made it necessary to revisit U.S. strategy by shifting attention back toward great power competition. As a result, the notion of strategic ambiguity became more widespread to maintain effective engagement and deterrence with competitors. The shift to the Indo-Pacific, in addition to the US support of regional allies and partners, illustrated US endeavors toward creating a conducive balance of power in vital theaters. Through these strains, consistent themes, such as respect for human rights, free trade, and multilateralism, have been a regular feature in America's strategic calculus—reflective of a commitment to supporting order based on international rules. In general, the strategic trajectory of America demonstrates an intricate blend of continuity and adaptation, representing a determination to protect its national interests and aspirations in the face of global volatility.

Key lessons from case studies

By dissecting two hooked case studies—Ukraine and the pivot to East Asia—we are given an understanding of the complexity behind America's ulterior grand strategy. The Ukraine war became a test of the U.S. strategic calculus, which seemed to be caught between regional alliances, balance of power, and geopolitical imperatives. This case study, carefully examined piecemeal, exposed the tangled interdependencies of American underwriting, European free rides, and the dynamics of balance-of-power politics. Also, the East Asia pivot, with its mixed narrative of Japan and China vs. the Indo-Pacific contest, had a good story about jockeying for position in a strategic space where you need to show teeth if you want Beijing deterred. These country studies also signify the dual aspects of U.S. involvement in world affairs and provide important lessons on balancing risks and opportunities in dual strategic contexts.

Exploring these case studies deepened our understanding of both the ethical and geopolitical roots that influence America's involvement abroad. These case studies allow us to deconstruct the complexities of America's strategic decision-making, sharpen our appreciation for the multiple levels of (in)coherence that characterize its choices, and highlight some of the potential downfalls as it seeks solutions on its existential journey. These case studies, in other words, typify the book's undertakings as cornerstones of knowledge that raise our consciousness about the labyrinthine factors behind America's secret grand design.

Articulation of Two Complementary Strategies

Hell, if we pound our way through the thick soupy fog of strategic and global chess that makes up our geopolitical challenge environment, this is revealing enough from the jump: The US has not one but two strategic hats on its head, with an explicit national security strategy riding cowpoke over a second semi-secret (crypto maybe?) grand strategy. The creation of these blueprint(s) requires that we critically analyze the comprehensive policy directives and military documents pertaining to foreign policy (and particularly their implications), as well as consult the positions of those seeking to be the authority on US geopolitical strategy. It is with this synthesis that we begin to see how the seen actions play out in relation to strategic calculi underlying U.S. foreign policy, which is a very messy enterprise.

At the center of this juxtaposition is the realization that though the NSS articulates immediate priorities and threats, behind it looms a covert grand strategy, which encompasses a far more pervasive longstanding vision for global influence and projection of power. Such dialectical dynamism allows for an understanding of how the convergence and divergence of these conceptual frameworks reveal different facets of American statecraft as simultaneously pragmatic and ambitious. And finally, the synthesis of these two frameworks allows us to see the complex trade-offs and concessions that national interest entails and how short-term requirements are weighed against long-term strategic purposes.

To that end, it is only by going beyond the level of what I have called "sloganeering" in U.S. foreign policy—and delving into its many nooks and crannies—that one can think broadly about the intricacies potentially driving military activism (or passivity) across region after region. At stake, finally, in the conjunctive construction of a pair of strategic frameworks is a system-wide prism through which to decode the complex fabric of American power politics and attain greater insight into the wider geopolitical landscape and motivations guiding U.S. relations with the world. From this perspective we can distill the patterns and recurrent themes that have always framed America's strategic praxis, looking ahead to its likely future and appraising what this may portend for principles of global stability and order. In breaking through the construction of those dual frames, we provide ourselves with the analytical apparatus needed to distinguish between forms in a contemporary international order.

Implications for International Order and Stability

The consequences of America having two strategic frames for international order and stability are profound, far-reaching, and subtle. Just as the United States grappled with a complicated world, so too did its strategic choices emanate across regions and time—influencing the distribution of power, structure of alliances, and balance between order and stability in the international system. A critical implication relates to the possibility of alignment as well as misalignment among powerful states, as the U.S. navigates its alliances and rivalries with strategic dexterity. Additionally, the way in which these strategies are pursued may serve to strengthen or weaken established international norms and institutions, and thus they contribute to defining what global order looks like.

America's choices have furthermore had a real impact on regional order and stability, especially in the key regions of the Indo-Pacific and Eastern Europe. How the U.S. deals with allies, confronts competition with adversaries, and grapples with the complexities of asymmetric threats is critically important in shaping these security landscapes. This in turn has spillover implications for the wider international order, not least because regional instabilities can have global consequences.

And also, the implications for international order and stability involve that fine line between assertiveness and leadership. Pursuing national interests while also adhering to international norms and principles has significant implications for the coherence and effectiveness of the world order. How the United States manages this delicate balance will define the future of global stability and great power rivalry.

Secondly, the ethical implications of America's secret grand design stretch and extend towards international order and stability. The manner in which the U.S. reconciles its strategic with its moral imperatives is not only indicative of the value it gives to these two considerations and to its credibility but also sends a signal to other actors in international politics about what is accepted and will be tolerated in the international sphere. The ethical consequences of American policies and behavior therefore should not be discounted when judging their effect on the world's peace.

In short, the consequences of the United States' deceitful strategic constructs for the world order and stability are far-reaching—they concern geopolitical equilibria, regional politics, and ethics, as well as the overall power equilibrium. It is crucial that policymakers, analysts, and stakeholders can appreciate these implications and are able to navigate the dimensions of their changing world in order to contribute to the development of an international system that is stable and prosperous.

Finding coherence in U.S. policies

"In reviewing so many facets of U.S. policy and U.S. actions on the world stage, we have asked what strategic logic would demand such a comprehensive approach, or modest response—non-strategic at times—that we see." At the core of such examination is the necessity for acknowledging the U.S. policies and their compatibility with its longer-term national interests and general geopolitical interests. This volume offers a detailed analysis of the diplomatic, economic, and military components of US policies, including not only reactions to immediate crises but also efforts to develop and implement strategies for the pursuit of long-term peace and stability.

By evaluating the convergence across various policy means and engagements, we can see the coherent orientation in practice and approach that defines the wider course of U.S. foreign relations. In addition, the development of US policies in history and its continuity and adaptation of core strategic principles offer useful information on the cohesiveness of long-term American grand strategy.

As we develop in this discussion, the multidimensionality of strategic coherence, while including its rational and intentional aspects as a constitutive element of the policymaking process, should also consider the complexity, trade-offs, and uncertainties more intrinsic to acting under conditions of change across regions and system levels. But it requires subtle analysis of the cross-cutting relationships among interests, values, and capabilities that drive U.S. policy and of the complex interaction between internal and external variables shaping its formation and pursuit.

Additionally, if we want to identify strategic coherence, it involves checking the fit between stated policy desires, real resources devoted to achieving these objectives, and the tactical means/ways by which this is done; it shows how theoretical or abstract intentions are realized in practice and operationalized. Central to such an analysis is the acknowledgement of the role that leadership, institutional arrangements, and policy processes play in the shaping of strategic coherence, capturing as it does the critical need for interagency coordination (Jones et al., 2016), stakeholder consultation (Fudge et al., 2012), and long-term planning (Berger & Luckmann, 1967) in aligning divergent policy strands into a single strategic framework.

This would include examining U.S. government policy coordination, efforts to build coherence among a range of policies and guidance, as well as results-focused reviews that underpin the structures and practices necessary for integrating all aspects of national security-related activities across the interagency to provide national-level strategic coherence. It also includes assessing the effectiveness of strategic communication, alliance management, and public diplomacy efforts in communicating and defending to external audiences the coherence of U.S. policies while building domestic support for those policies.

The search for coherence in U.S. strategy is both an exercise in self-evaluation and adaptation—one of the marks of a great power—but also an important factor influencing global expectations, perceptions, and responses to American leadership and activism. By more successfully locating and explaining strategic coherence, the United States can seek to foster greater predictability, credibility, and trust in its international relations—which in turn would improve Washington's ability to influence and manage the highly interconnected yet competitive global landscape. Disentangling the strands of strategic consistency in U.S. policy is thus a necessary project to understanding, assessing, and resetting the strategic dimensions of American global leadership.

Risks and Pitfalls to Avoid

The concept of strategic overreach, counterintuitive as it might appear to the study of international relations theoreticians, rings a bell when considering potential adverse implications and negative fallout lurking behind the U.S. global strategic architecture. This dynamic involves the stretching of resources, influence, and military involvement to unsustainable limits that threaten overarching strategic objectives. The difficulties associated with strategic overreach must be approached with prudence; its consequences can resonate on geopolitical terrains, bringing about unforeseen challenges and systemic vulnerabilities.

Strategic overreach becomes the risk of confrontation when the level of reasonable engagement is surpassed. The desire of a nation for global leadership and hegemony might plant the seeds of discord, generate enmity, and provoke counterbalances from other poles, making geopolitical rivalries more acute and precipitating frictions. In addition, the financial and human capital costs associated with far-reaching projects may give rise to domestic dissatisfaction and socio-economic conflicts, which would erode societal resilience and unity.

As a part of the United States's hidden grand plot, strategic overstretch has multidimensional risks that require intelligent watching. For one, unlimited and long-term military deployments stretch the nation's monetary and human resources to breaking point, siphoning a valuable focus and money from vital domestic needs like roads, schools, and hospitals. And secondly, the loss of diplomatic credibility and moral authority could be associated with the perception that efforts to breach restraints are making rapid progress or provoke international reactions (what one could also call "diplomatic blowback"), undermining this portion of diplomacy's substratum, which has a multiplier effect on trust in global relations.

The third way…'This is not to say that the West's mission is only or mainly humanitarian in Syria; were it so, there would be no point sending planes to bomb IS and other nasty Islamist groups.' Entering protracted, unwinnable asymmetrical conflicts can exacerbate local insecurity and blur the crucial line between necessary intervention and expansion, supported by European entrepreneurial billionaires. Complex issue linkages and domino effects in regional dynamics can multiply the dangers, leading perhaps to quicksand that ties the country down helplessly and corrodes its advantages as well as leverage. Further, the combined consequences of strategic overreach may echo across the world, dragging on international organizations, compounding regional anxieties, and causing collateral damage in neighboring states.

To confront the specter of strategic overreach will require a subtle balance between active involvement and healthy skepticism about world affairs. It requires sound strategic foresight, sophisticated policy calibration, and flexibility in response to changing international conditions. It also highlights the value of strong interagency cooperation from diverse and skilled professionals in dealing with this world's complexities with scalpel-like accuracy and judgement."

In other words, defining the parameters of strategic overreach is key to protecting the long-term national interest and reorienting strategic postures. American strategy at this decisive juncture may thus thread the needle of audacious aspiration and prudent prudence, transcending predicaments of overreach in service of resilient and principled global leadership that is defined by the enduring activities of statesmanly success and aligned national interests.

Ethical Issues in the Conduct of Strategy

In the domains of international relations and strategy, morality has been cast in a central role concerning the behavior of nation-states. While the US pursues its hidden grand design and dual strategic frameworks, it faces difficult moral considerations related to exercising power in the international arena. A significant issue, and one that I would like to focus on for a moment tonight, is the question: under what conditions can war be considered just? The principles of this theory require measured judgement on the proportionality of military action, distinction between combatant and non-combatant targets, and the legitimacy of a just cause for intervention.

Moreover, ethical deliberation is necessary to consider the side effects and unintended consequences of strategic endeavors. This requires a sincere consideration of the potential human price tag that comes with geopolitical tactics and military operations. Besides, strategic dimensions of decision-making also have ethical ones, such as human rights advocacy, global suffering, and peace development. But these are points that emphasize states' moral obligation to the well-being and dignity of persons, regardless of geopolitics.

In the light of America's concealed grand strategy, these ethics reflections are essential to assess the strategic consequences over time of strategic decisions, notably when it comes to alliances and intervening or using force. Proactively anticipating and minimizing potential humanitarian disasters, addressing the needs of vulnerable populations that are displaced, and demonstrating respect for international norms and conventions are key aspects of ethical behavior in strategic choice. In addition, these ethics are not limited to consequences—they operate across time as well (ethical decisions we make affect future people and global policy). I think that requires us to have some kind of forward-looking ethical vision that moves beyond advances in political strategies to consider the lasting moral legacy of U.S. strategic decisions.

As the United States balances its national interest with moral imperative, it seeks to find balance in the integration of power and principle in pursuit of security and stability around the world. By "thinking ethically in America's foreign policy," we mean that the application of ethics to policy provides more morally defensible and sustainable policies as well as aid to promoting a fair, humane, and decent world order—one that embodies universal ethical norms according to which all nations should be treated.

Future Lessons for Security and Diplomacy

Unpacking the complex balance between morals, national interest, diplomacy tactics, and security imperatives exposes some valuable lessons that can be used as guiding posts on charts charting a course through today's ever-complicating world stage. One key lesson is the need for nuanced thinking that takes account of short-term national interest and long-run global responsibility. Managing these sometimes-conflicting objectives requires shrewd diplomacy, forward-thinking strategic instincts, and a practical grasp of changing geopolitical realities.

Prospective security and diplomatic endeavors should stress the need for multilateral involvement and coalition formation. In an age of transnational issues, whether terrorism, pandemics, or climate change, the effectiveness of unilateral decisions is inherently limited. Coordinated efforts that leverage the combined resources, knowledge, and capabilities of compatible nations can lead to more effective, sustainable responses to shared threats and challenges.

This book's narratives highlighted the crucial need for empathy, cultural awareness, and inclusive communication in formulating successful security and diplomatic measures. Being sensitive to different interpretations and recognizing historical layers and local perspectives is key for trust building, cooperation, and avoiding tensions that might degenerate into confrontations. Therefore, it is important to have a body of diplomats and strategists skilled in cultural nuance and human coalition to develop and maintain global peace.

Moreover, the experiences derived from the case studies in previous chapters emphasize the importance of flexibility and agility to react towards emergent security threats. A dynamic security- and diplomacy-oriented approach is needed in light of the fast-paced technology development, an increase in asymmetric threats, and changing alliances. Technological innovation, the use of state-of-the-art intelligence-gathering means, and the application of modern technological tools for positive non-coercive influence are essential elements of forward-looking approaches.

The examination of both historical models and present-day examples highlights the relevance of consistent, principle-based leadership with ethical and moral underpinnings. Those in positions of leadership who are shaping the security and diplomatic response to terrorism have big choices: they ought to operate unencumbered by the mundane form constraints and pursue a path that upholds universal values and supports human rights, not in thrall to expediency and short-termism. However, by maintaining a strong adherence to ethical behavior and principled statecraft as the foundation for future action, states can chart out a better and more secure world.

Balancing National Interest and Global Responsibility

In the anarchy of international relations, balancing national interests and global obligations is a taxing issue for even leaders who have to take decisions, perhaps most so for those in Washington. The compulsion to defend and prosper your nation is symbolic of the sovereign story of every nation-state, including matters related to security, economic development, and societal welfare. But in a world that has long been interconnected with transnational threats and shared problems, there is a strong case for weighing such exclusive national self-interest against wider global obligations.

For the US, this tightrope walk is often manifest in its foreign policies that balance between serving its own needs and fulfilling its function as world leader. Finding this balance necessitates a nuanced strategy that takes into account the immediate effects of unilateralist steps on the rest of the world but also secures long-term strategic advantage for such a country.

We need to have a complex perception of the inextricable linkedness that exists between national interests and global responsibilities. The United States, therefore, must understand that our national security and economic well-being are intertwined with the stability and success of other countries. Solving global problems, such as climate change, pandemics, and terrorism, demands a collaborative and multilateralist approach that recognizes the interdependence of countries. And the search for strategic interests requires an understanding of the consequences of American policies on the international system, along with a wish to help create a favorable global climate for peace, security, and development. This therefore leads into the necessity to balance domestic interests with global responsibilities, which in turn ensures that when it does take a lead on issues—as most recently has been, of course, with ISIS and Iraq—then it's also thinking about, 'What is the impact not only for us?' But what signals by our actions are we sending out around the world? It is in this context that it will be indispensable to make use of its influence and strength to resolve international crises, seek ways towards diplomatic solutions, and provide for the principle of collective security.

Yet the fine line is not so simple as the world becomes more connected. Challenges remain in reconciling national priorities and global responsibilities, with conflicting government objectives and systemic limitations impeding attempts to reconcile the two sets of responses. This requires delicate tuning of both policies and engagements so that national interests are pursued without taking the focus off global welfare. It takes finesse to find that sweet spot, diplomacy to negotiate it, and hard coalition work to build a structure that seeks the best for its nation while being positive contributors to the global village. It takes recognizing that pursuing one's narrow self-interest instead of fostering greater worldwide stability will ultimately serve to undermine the interests of every nation, including America.

As the world evolves, the need for America to balance its own interests and responsibilities in a new global order remains an abiding principle of its foreign policy. To best negotiate this complex landscape, development and implementation of U.S. strategies should be guided by a balanced mixture of pragmatism, principle, and long-term vision. With such a guideline, America can exercise its international interests systematically and responsibly and contribute to building a world order in which all countries are partners with mutual benefit, cooperation, and prosperity.

Closing Thoughts: Dealing with a Complicated Geopolitical Landscape

Understanding the labyrinthine web of international geopolitics requires a keen understanding of the difficulties and interactions that govern international politics. From an analysis of how America has shaped this landscape, we can see that the pursuit of national interests must be qualified by broader global responsibilities. This fine balance requires a nuanced standpoint that appreciates the compulsions of national security and yet the importance of respecting international order. A retrospective of these social obligations closes the volume with a reflection on its complexity and on hurdles as well as potentials ahead.

In a time when the world is experiencing rapid geopolitics and the balance of power is changing, the US must have a strategic stance that takes into consideration the interaction between the interests of many forces in the world. The ascent of new regional powers, a remobilization of old great powers, and the entry onto the stage of non-state actors have rearranged the map of the world. You have to be able to dance through this complex landscape and understand the overlapping goals and aspirations of the communities that live there.

The changing face of the world's geopolitics also requires a rethinking of our old ideas of what security and diplomacy entail. Given that we're on the cusp of meeting numerous transnational challenges, from climate change to terrorism to pandemics, it's clear we need a more comprehensive vision that goes far beyond national self-interest. This demands a cooperative and inclusive manner of global problem-solving, articulating the interdependence of our globe and the joint international obligation to combat common threats.

And in addition, the U.S. must be aware of all the moral implications of its behavior in the world arena. Indeed, as the defender of liberal democratic values and human rights norms, America's behavior has ripple effects that extend to every corner of the globe. That is why it requires a deft hand to navigate such complex geopolitical terrain, and in doing so, it would be ideal that the principles transcending national interest are adhered to. Adhering to moral clarity in a world where others wave away such responsibilities is not simply the means by which America serves its interests in the world, but how there can be such a thing as an international order that is stable and just.

In sum, the complexities of today's geopolitical environment make it necessary to rethink America's grand strategy in its entirety. Mastering their [China, Ukraine, and Russia] complex interface requires not just smart diplomatic and military footwork but also deep knowledge of the ethical values and changing paradigms of global governance. In adopting this multidimensional approach, the United States may be able to engage the complexities of the global arena with wisdom, prudence, and dedication to promoting a more secure, prosperous, and harmonious world.

www.ingramcontent.com/pod-product-compliance
Lightning Source LLC
Chambersburg PA
CBHW020532080526
44583CB00013B/829